SYSTEMATIC THEOLOGY
The Seven Pillars
The Plan of Salvation

SYSTEMATIC THEOLOGY

THE SEVEN PILLARS

THE PLAN OF SALVATION

NYRON MEDINA

Systematic Theology: The Seven Pillars , The Plan of Salvation
First Edition 2017

All inquiries should be addressed to:

Thusia Seventh Day Adventist Church
Romain Lands, Lady Young Road,
Morvant
Trinidad and Tobago
Telephone #: 1-868-625-0446

Unless otherwise indicated, Scripture quotations are from the King James Version of the Bible.

ISBN-13:978-1976279522
ISBN-10: 1976279526

Front cover designed by Dell Medina

www.thusiasdaevangel.com

"Wisdom hath builded her house, she hath hewn out her seven pillars" **Proverbs 9:1**

A Publication of Thusia Seventh Day Adventist Church

Printed in the United States of America

CONTENTS

Introduction vii

The Godhead 1

The Depravity of Man 7

Providential Grace (The Merits) 13

Prevenient Grace (The Calling) 23

Renewing Grace (Justification) 29

Imparted Grace (Sanctification) 39

Judicial Grace (Investigative Judgment & the Blotting out)45

SYSTEMATIC THEOLOGY (1986 Edition)............................ 65

About The Author 107

NOTES 111

Introduction

THEOLOGY IS OUR STUDY OF GOD; but it also encompasses our study of God as it relates to sinful man. Theology is systematic because it comprehends the orderly works of God who will not justify a man without first having provisions to do so. Thus systematic theology explains the perfect order of God's Plan of Salvation or Atonement for the sake of helping man to understand the real science of salvation with its connecting links of truth related to truth. This revelation is absolutely important for the procedural organization of man's consciousness of divine reality so that his life experience may be organized and be a comprehensive blessing to all in a world of error and confusion. We use the word revelation with regards to systematic theology, because man's study of God is worthless without the revelation of the Holy Spirit. Only God can reveal God, so that the theological positions of any systematic theology must be the supernatural revelation of God to those that seek, knock and ask.

Systematic theology has revealed to us the gross mistakes of the theologians of the past who have mixed up justification with the judgment and have unnaturally divided justification and sanctification to cause one to be devoid of the power of God, and the other to be inefficient in truly delivering sinners from sin. The light of God coming from the second apartment of the heavenly sanctuary is the light of systematic theology after 1844, and it begins with the judgment going way back to the Godhead.

May all be blessed by this end time light in Jesus' name, Amen.

THE GODHEAD

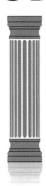

1.   Everything begins with God, He was before all things, He, is the uncreated. Colossians 1:17.

2.   God is God in nature, that is, in being and make up. Galatians 4:8.

3.   In the Bible God is identified as the following characteristics:

    i.   One. Galatians 3:20.

    ii.   Invisible. Colossians 1:15.

    iii.   Divine. 2 Peter 1:4.

    iv.   Spirit. John 4:24.

    v.   Nature. (2 Peter 1:4; Galatians 4:8).

    vi.   Love. 1 John 4:8, 16.

THE CHARACTERISTICS OF GOD
I. GOD IS ONE – Galatians 3:20. II. GOD IS INVISIBLE – Colossians 1:15. III. GOD IS DIVINE – 2 Peter 1:4. IV. GOD IS SPIRIT – John 4:24. V. GOD IS GOD IN NATURE – (2 Peter 1:4. Galatians 4:8). VI. GOD IS LOVE – 1 John 4:8,16.

Figure (1) A diagram of the characteristics of God.

4. God is described as being in three persons. The persons are not God, but God is in the persons.

   a. Here is the fact of the three persons. Isaiah 48:12,16,17; Matthew 3:16,17; 1 John 5:7.

   b. God is IN the persons, because this is how Jesus showed the indwelling to be. 2 Corinthians 5:19; Colossians 2:9.

5. The Divine Nature dwells in the persons in the offices of Will, Mediator, and Creative Agency. These offices are divine offices since they are the offices of the one Divine Nature – God.

   c. Office of Will. Galatians 1:4.

   d. Office of Mediator. Hebrews 8:6.

   e. Office of Creative Agency. Malachi 2:10.

THE OFFICES OF GOD

I.   OFFICE OF WILL – Galatians 1:4.
II. OFFICE OF MEDIATOR – Hebrews 8:6.
III. OFFICE OF CREATIVE AGENCY – Malachi 2:10.

Figure (2) A diagram of the Offices of God.

6. Another important unchangeable fact is the order of revelation from the one Divine Nature in the three persons. They are:

    a. The one Divine Nature reveals Himself as Will in the first person called the Father. Matthew 7:21.

    b. The one Divine Nature reveals Himself as Mediator (Revealer) in the second person called the Son. 1 Timothy 2:5.

    c. The one Divine Nature reveals Himself as Creative Agency in the third person called the Holy Spirit. Psalm 104:30.

7. Another important fact is that the Divine Nature, God Himself, is sometimes called Father.

    a. The first person is called Father, i.e. Father Person. (The Divine Nature in the Father Person). John 17:1; 1 John 5:7.

    b. The Divine Nature, God Himself, is called Father, i.e. Divine Father Nature (Father Divine Nature). John 17:21; Isaiah 9:6; John 10:30.

8. The Holiness of God shows that He is unique and way above all (that is, His creation). He is so because He alone is God. Thus the holiness of God is His God-onlyness. 1 Samuel 2:2; Exodus

15:11.

9.   There are two entities alone in God's Universe. They are:

     a.   God. James 2:19.

     b.   Creation. Romans 8:22.

10.   Reality in the Universe shows that creation can never be the Creator, because God is God alone. Psalm 86:8-10.

11.   God reveals Himself by His name YHWH; this is the name of the Divine Nature. Isaiah 42:8; Exodus 3:15.

12.   YHWH is one YHWH. Deuteronomy 6:4.

13.   Jesus name in the Hebrew reveals Him to be the one Divine Nature who is Saviour in a temple of human flesh. He is called YAH-SHUA. (Matthew 1:21; Isaiah 43:11).

14.   The Law of God, the Ten Commandments has two sides. They are:

     a.   The law of works side. Romans 3:20.

     b.   The Spiritual Law side. Romans 7:14.

15.   It is not God that was meant to reveal the Law, but rather the Law was meant to reveal God.

     a.   The Law is holy because God is holy. (Leviticus 11:44; Leviticus 19:2; Romans 7:12).

     b.   The Law is just because God is just. Deuteronomy 32:4; Isaiah 45:21; Romans 7:12).

     c.   The Law is good because God is good. (Matthew 19:17; Psalm 119:68; Romans 7:12).

16. Thus the Spiritual Law is a revelation of the Nature of God; it reveals the principles of His Divine Nature. Here are the principles that make up the Law of the Ten Commandments, revealing God's Nature.

    i. God is God. Psalm 86:10.

    ii. God is Glory. Psalm 29:2,3; Isaiah 42:8.

    iii. God is Will. John 6:38; Philippians 2:13.

    iv. God is Creator. 1 Peter 4:19.

    v. God is Life. John 14:6; 1 John 5:20.

    vi. God is Saviour. Isaiah 43:11.

    vii. God is Eternal. 1 Timothy 1:17.

    viii. God is Grace. 1 Peter 5:10.

    ix. God is Truth. Deuteronomy 32:4.

    x. God is Righteousness. Jeremiah 23:6.

THE SPIRITUAL LAW

I. GOD IS GOD - Psalm 86:10.

II. GOD IS GLORY - Psalm 29:2, 3. Isaiah 42:8.

III. GOD IS WILL - John 6:38. Philippians 2:13.

IV. GOD IS CREATOR- 1 Peter 4:19.

V. GOD IS LIFE - John 14:6. 1 John 5:20.

VI. GOD IS SAVIOR - Isaiah 43:11.

VII. GOD IS ETERNAL-1 Timothy 1:17.

VIII. GOD IS GRACE-1 Peter 5:10.

IX. GOD IS TRUTH - Deuteronomy 32:4.

X. GOD IS RIGHTEOUSNESS - Jeremiah 23:6.

Figure (3) A diagram on the Spiritual Law.

17. Put together, the Spiritual Law is Love, that is, principled Love. 1 John 4:7-12.

18. This is what it means when we say God is Love; God is principled Love, God is indeed the Spiritual Law. (1 John 4:16; 1 John 3:17,18).

THE DEPRAVITY OF MAN

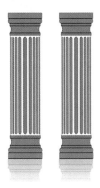

1. In the beginning God created man in His **image** after His likeness. Genesis 1:26,27.

2. The **Image** of God is always **God Himself** in the creature or person.

    a. Jesus was the **image** of the invisible God. Colossians 1:15; 2 Corinthians 4:4.

    b. God was in the **body** of Christ. 2 Corinthians 5:19; Colossians 2:9.

3. Thus man who was created with God – the Divine Nature – in him, was created **sinfree**. (Psalm 25:8; Ecclesiastes 7:29); Colossians 3:10.

4. The likeness that God created man in was like **His person**, having a body form like the Father and Son. (Genesis 1:26; Daniel 7:9,13; Revelation 1:13-16).

5. Man was created to glorify God which is to exalt Him to be God

alone. (Isaiah 43:1,7; Psalm 29:2; Psalm 86:9,10).

6. When man fell into sin, it was over claiming that there were **Gods with God** as Lucifer claimed in the beginning of his rebellion. (Isaiah 14:12-14; Genesis 3:1-6).

7. This sin however caused man to **lose** the Divine Nature or **image of God** from within him, he became **Vacuous** or **emptied of God**. This is the beginning of the Depravity of man. (Ephesians 2:12; Romans 1:28; Ephesians 4:17,18).

8. The Depravity of Man as a result of sin is expressed in certain legitimate ways.

   a. Emptied of God (Vacuous state).

   b. Having the **Carnal Mind** or **Idol Values** in the heart.

   c. Having the **Body of Sins** or **Perverted Emotions**.

   d. Having **Evil Practices** or **Sinful Works**.

   e. Having **Sinful Flesh**.

      i. Sinful Flesh is flesh **infected with sin** and flesh **affected by sin**, or **only** flesh **affected by sin** (as in the case of Jesus).

      ii. Sinful Flesh is flesh that has **Infirmities**.

      iii. Sinful Flesh is flesh that has **Liabilities** of perverted emotions flowing in it.

   f. **Infirmities** of the sinful flesh are **weaknesses** of the flesh **affected by sin**.

      i. They are bodily weaknesses of hunger, thirst, weariness and a **weakened constitution**.

ii. They are also **habits** or **moral weaknesses** not necessarily practiced.

9. On page (12) the figure (1) chart explains the **Depravity** of Man.

10. It was Adam that made us sinners. Romans 5:12,19.

11. Because, it was because of his **original sinning** in the Garden of Eden that Adam caused us to be **alienated from God** from the **womb**, or to be **born** without **God**. Psalm 51:5; Psalm 58:3; Isaiah 48:8.

12. Without God, creation becomes God to man, so that he naturally adopts **idols in the mind**. This is **idol-values** that is called the **thought of the flesh** or the **Carnal Mind**. Ezekiel 14:3-5; Romans 8:6-8.

13. Since it is our minds that evoke feelings, emotions, or passions, with the Carnal mind in the unconverted, his **perverted emotions** (called the body of sins) flow, gratifying him. Romans 6:6,12; Romans 7:5,8.

14. Next follows **works** of **sinning** or sinful works. (Isaiah 59:6-8; Micah 7:2,3; Galatians 5:19-21).

15. When Adam sinned, his children received **biological inheritances** from him and also **influencive inheritances**, so that, being without God, they inherited flesh **infected by sin** (no God within) and thus **affected by sin** (as infirmities). Romans 5:12,18,19.

16. Sinful man has **sinful flesh infected with sin**. Romans 7:18,8.

17. But **sinful flesh** as our **inheritance biologically** is **not** sin, because it is flesh affected by sin, not infected **with** sin. Jesus had our **sinful flesh**, yet He was **without** sin. (Romans 8:3; 1 John 3:5).

18.   Sinful flesh **itself** is **not sin**; it is flesh that has **infirmities** (we call it **neutral infirmities**). These infirmities are like, hunger, weariness, thirst and a general **weakened bodily constitution**, in **intellectual strength** and **muscular strength**. (Romans 8:26; Matthew 8:17; 2 Corinthians 12:5,9).

19.   Infirmities are also **moral infirmities**, that is, **moral weaknesses** or **habits** that are **not practiced**. Habits are in those that are sinfree, but the habits are **not practiced**, but are **dormant** in the unconscious mind. While these habits are **sinful**, they are not sin to the person until he **practices** them. Hebrews 4:15; Hebrews 5:2.

20.   Sinful flesh is also flesh that has the **liabilities** of **perverted emotions** flowing in the body, but they are kept as **liabilities** and are not allowed to be removed from that category to become **actualities**. Romans 6:12.

21.   Jesus had **human depravity** in the fact that He had **flesh** depraved by sin which is **sinful flesh**, but this is not sin. (Romans 8:3; Philippians 2:7; Hebrews 2:14).

22.   **Human Nature** is made up of the following:

   i.   Thoughts.

   ii.   Emotions.

   iii.   Flesh.

23.   To say the term **sinful human nature** is therefore to speak about the following:

   a.   **Thoughts** infected with sin. Genesis 6:5.

   b.   **Emotions**, desires, passions directed by sin. Genesis 3:6.

   c.   Thus flesh **infected with** sin. Romans 7:18.

24.   But man can have **sinfree human nature**. This is:

a.   Thoughts **without sin**. (Psalm 119:11; Psalm 37:31).

b.   Emotions **not directed by sin**. Colossians 2:11; Romans 6:12.

c.   Sinful flesh yet without sin. 1 John 3:9; 1 John 5:18.

25.   Initially **no** man is **righteous inherently**. Romans 3:9-19.

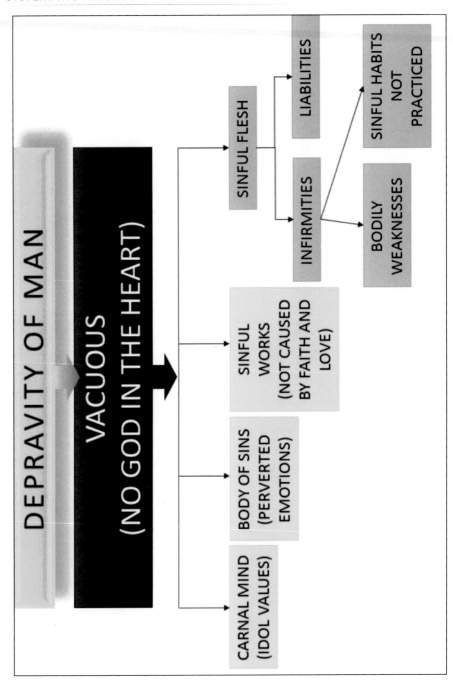

Figure (1) A diagram on the Depravity of Man.

Providential Grace (The Merits)

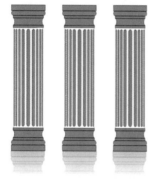

1. The Divine Nature, God, looking at the **depravity of man** produces a **vision** called the **Plan of Salvation**; the **Whole Atonement** (Reconciliation) or the **Whole Grace of God**. (John 3:16-18; John 1:12-14; 2 John 9); 2 Corinthians 9:8; 2 Timothy 1:9,10; 1 Peter 5:10.

2. This Plan of Salvation or Whole Atonement is made up of **five points of Grace**. The following chart shows this to us.

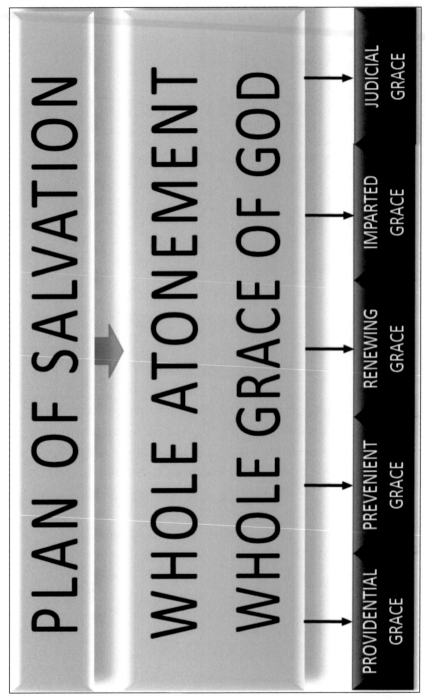

Figure (1) A diagram on the Five Points of Grace.

3. Using **Justification** as the **change centre** of the **Plan of Salvation**, each of the points of Grace can be described surrounding **Justification**.

    i.   **Providential Grace**: The **foundations** of Justification.

    ii. **Prevenient Grace**: The **conditions** of Justification.

    iii. **Renewing Grace**: The **means** of Justification.

    iv. **Imparted Grace**: The **results** of Justification.

    v.   **Judicial Grace**: The **end** of Justification.

4. The term **Providential Grace** is **monergistic**-that means that it is **provided** by **God alone**, and by no part of any creation in **any** sense. This is the same as saying that salvation is **not by works**. (Ephesians 2:8,9; Isaiah 43:11,12).

5. **Providential Grace** itself has five **constituents**. This means that **five necessities** are provided by God to save sinful man. The following chart illustrates:

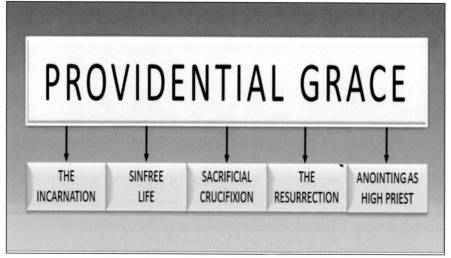

Figure (2) is a diagram of Providential Grace.

6. **Three parts** of Providential Grace are called the **Humiliation of**

Christ, because Jesus had to **humble** Himself to perform them. The following chart shows us.

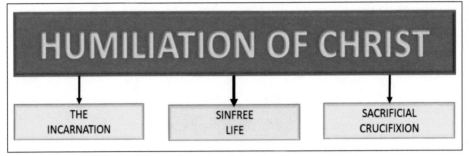

Figure (3) is a diagram of the Humiliation of Christ.

7. Here is the **logic** of the points of Providential Grace.

    a. Christ came in human flesh to get rid of sin, this is why Christ **incarnated**. (Matthew 1:18-25; John 1:1,10-13; Hebrews 2:14-18).

    b. Jesus lived a **sinfree life** to take away sin. (1 John 3:5; 1 Peter 1:18-20).

    c. Jesus died a **sacrificial death** in His **crucifixion** that we might be made free from sin. (1 Peter 2:21-24; Galatians 1:3,4; Titus 2:13,14; Galatians 3:1).

    d. If Jesus did not **resurrect**, we are yet in our sins, thus His **resurrection** was meant to rid us of our sins. (1 Corinthians 15:14-17; Romans 6:5-9).

    e. Jesus was **anointed** as **High Priest** over the Heavenly Sanctuary to minister for us to be made sinfree. (Hebrews 2:17; Hebrews 6:19,20; Hebrews 8:1-3).

8. The **logic** of the three points of the **Humiliation of Christ** is as follows.

    a. Jesus humiliated Himself to come in the flesh of man **affected by sin** for thousands of years. He incarnated into **sinful flesh**. (Romans 8:3; Philippians 2:6-8).

b.   Jesus had to depend on God to **fight infirmities** to live a **sinfree life**. In this He humbled Himself. (Hebrews 5:7-9; Hebrews 2:18).

c.   Dying an **ignominious death** as **public crucifixion** while suffering for man's sins and giving him eternal life was indeed humiliating. (Hebrews 2:6,7,9; Acts. 8:32,33).

9.   The **Incarnation** is explained as two points. This following chart illustrates.

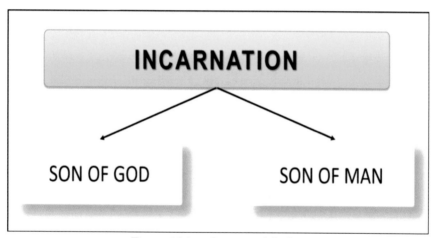

Figure (4) is a diagram of the Incarnation.

a.   **Son of God** means a son (a **begotten** one) who is God. Hebrews 1:5,6.

b.   Son of God means that **Jesus is God**. Hebrews 1:8-12.

c.   This means that the **divinity** that was in the **human body** of Jesus was His **divine identity**. (2 Corinthians 5:19; Colossians 2:9; John 8:24,58).

d.   **Son of Man** means that Jesus was a son of Adam or a son of the **human family**. He was a **real human being**. (Daniel 7:13; Matthew 1:1; Luke 3:23,38).

e.   This means that Jesus was **man** as humans are humanity. 1 Timothy 2:5; Matthew 8:20.

10.   As **Son of Man** in **human flesh**, Jesus had **sinful human flesh**. This means He had human flesh **affected by sin**. Romans 8:3; Philippians 2:7,8.

a.   Jesus had **no sin**, thus He was not **infected with sin**. 1 Peter 2:21,22.

11.   Having **sinful human flesh** means that Jesus had **infirmities** and **liabilities**. The following chart illustrates.

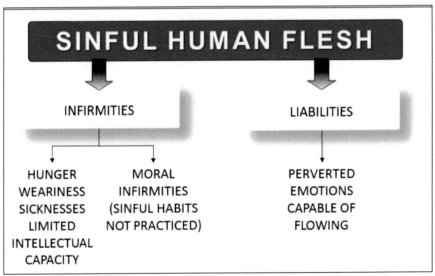

Figure (5) is a diagram of Sinful Human Flesh.

a.   That Jesus had **infirmities** can clearly be seen. Hebrews 4:15.

b.   The fact that Jesus inherited **Moral Infirmities** can be judged from the **notorious lineage** He had. (Hebrews 2:16; Luke 3:27; Matthew 1:12; Luke 3:31,32; Matthew

1:4-6).

c.   **Perverted emotions** could flow in Jesus once He was not in subjection to the Will of God. Matthew 26:36-45.

12.   The **Sacrificial Crucifixion** shows that the crucifixion of Jesus by the Romans and Jews had **spiritual realities** behind it, realities that were a **spiritual sacrifice**. (1 Corinthians 1:23,24; 1 Corinthians 2:2; Galatians 2:20; Ephesians 5:2; 1 Corinthians 5:7; Hebrews 9:26; Hebrews 10:12).

13.   The **Sacrificial Crucifixion** is made up of two parts. The following chart illustrates.

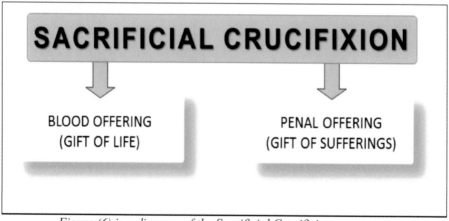

Figure (6) is a diagram of the Sacrificial Crucifixion.

14.   When Jesus lived upon the earth He was a man of sorrows acquainted with grief showing that His whole life has **sufferings** for man's sins in it. Isaiah 53:3,10.

15.   The **penalty** He **experienced** on the cross was **sufferings** for man's sins unto **death**. Hebrews 2:9,10; 1 Peter 3:18.

16.   This is the **Penal Offering** He made available on the cross to give man a **consciousness** of the **infinite horribleness** of, and

God's hate for sin. 1 Peter 4:1,2.

17. It is this offering that evokes **genuine** repentance in man that God can forgive him. 2 Corinthians 7:9-11.

18. In the Bible **blood** symbolizes **Life**. Leviticus 17:11,14; Deuteronomy 12:23.

19. The **blood offering** is the **gift of Life** made available as a gift of God on the cross. John 10:10,11,15; John 3:14-16; Romans 6:23.

20. Life is an **experience** of the **Love of God** (called a knowledge of God and Christ). John 17:3.

21. It is this **Life** that is given to **dwell** in man as a **substitute** replacing spiritual death. Ephesians 2:2,5; 1 John 3:15; Romans 8:10,11.

22. Christ **died for us** means that He died to bring us to God (thus ending our alienation from God), by making us become conscious of the horribleness of sin (through a consciousness of the sufferings of Christ given to our minds by the Spirit), that we may repent and believe to receive the **gift of life** in the **heart,** in place of the idol values, by **Justification**. (1 Peter 2:24, 25; 1 Peter 3:18; Romans 8:6; Romans 5:1).

23. Thus the **death of Christ** we call a **subjective substitution in intention**. This means that the death of Christ is meant to cause a **subjective exchange experience** that **converts** the penitent man. 2 Corinthians 5:14,15; Titus 2:13,14.

24. It is the **Sacrificial Crucifixion** we explain as the **death of Christ**. And it is the **death of Christ** that means His **Sufferings** (the Penal Offering) and His **Gift of Life** (the Blood Offering). 1 Peter 3:18; John 10:11,15.

25. Then in **Providential Grace** we have what is called the **exaltation of Christ**. The following chart explains.

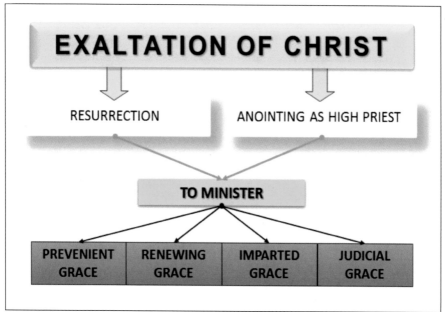

Figure (7) is a diagram of the Exaltation of Christ.

26. Jesus' resurrection was glorious and exalted Him as the **Firstborn from the dead** (that is, as the resurrected One upon whom the resurrection of all depends), thus He stands out above all other men that are resurrected. Colossians 1:17-19.

27. Jesus is exalted by being anointed as High Priest in the **order of Melchisedec**, (that is, a priest with no beginning or ending). (Hebrews 5:8-10; Hebrews 6:19,20; Hebrews 7:1-10,15-17,21,22).

28. Jesus' **Priesthood** is **continual** (daily). Hebrews 7:23,24.

29. Jesus' **Ministry** is **continual** (daily). Hebrews 7:25-28.

30. **Providential Grace** is therefore the Grace of God as a **provision** made available for the redemption of man. (Genesis 22:8; John

1:29; John 3:16).

31.   **Providential Grace** is called the **Merits of Salvation**, or Graces we did not earn, but were made available for man by God's Grace. (Romans 5:20,21; Romans 4:4,16).

32.   The following illustrated Chart explains:

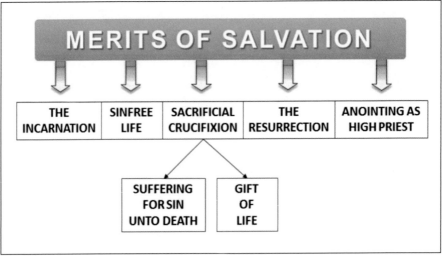

Figure 8 is a diagram of the Merits of Salvation.

Prevenient Grace (The Calling)

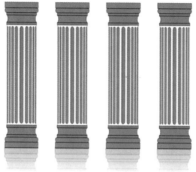

1. The **Whole Grace of God** or the **Plan of Salvation** can be divided into **two parts** expressing **purpose**. They are **Provision** and **Application**. The following chart explains.

2 CORINTHIANS 9:8

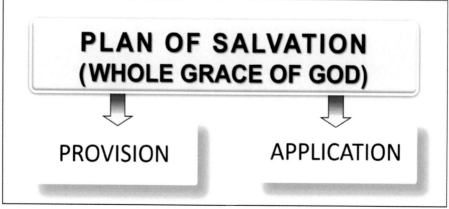

Figure 1 is a diagram of the Plan of Salvation.

a. God **provides** the **sacrifice**. Genesis 22:8.

b.   But the **provision** must also be **applied**. Exodus 24:6-8.

2.   The facts are that the points under **Providential Grace** (the Merits) are **provisions**, while the rest of Graces are **applications**. The following chart shows.

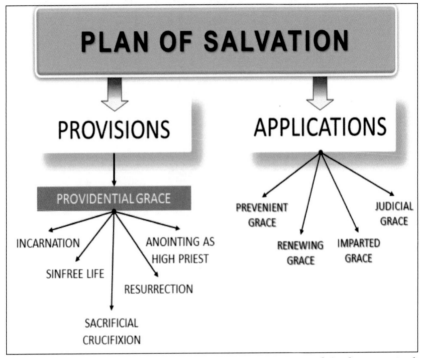

Figure (2) A diagram of the components of the Provisions and Applications in the Plan of Salvation.

3.   **Applications** are the use of **Merits** by God's salvific action as **antidote** to apply to man's problem of sin. (Hebrews 9:18-22; Hebrews 10:11-13,21,22).

4.   The very **first application** of the Plan of Salvation is **Prevenient Grace** or Grace to **call** man to God. Romans 9:11; 1 Corinthians 1:24; Romans 8:28.

5.   God by His Spirit uses the **Sacrificial Crucifixion** or the **Death of Christ** to call men. John 12:32,33.

6.   Prevenient Grace is made up of the following points. See chart below.

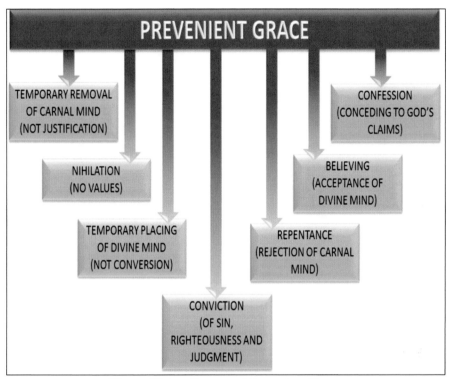

Figure (3) is a diagram of Prevenient Grace.

7.   Prevenient Grace is **synergistic**, that means parts are done by **God** and parts are done by **man** under divine **influence**. The chart on page (30), figure (4) illustrates this reality.

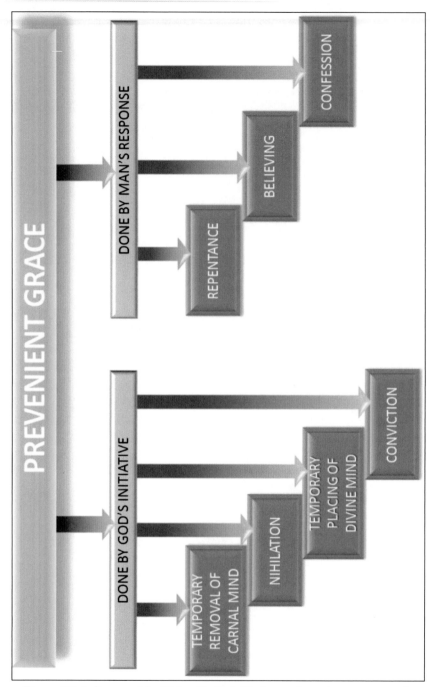

Figure (4) A diagram identifying God's initiative and man's response under Prevenient Grace.

8. God **first** calls man, this is His **monergistic initiative**. 1 Thessalonians 4:7; 1 Thessalonians 5:24; Ephesians 4:4.

9. Man's **penitence** is his response to **God's calling**. Acts 9:3-12.

10. **Temporary removal of the Carnal Mind**: Since the Carnal Mind is not subject to the Law of God it cannot see truth. We need God's light to see light, thus the Carnal Mind must be **temporarily removed**. (Romans 8:6-8; Psalm 36:9).

11. **Nihilation (no values):** The very **brief moment** the **carnal mind** is **removed**, and just **before** the **divine mind** is temporarily placed in the person's mind, this is a period of **no values** (Nihilation). Acts 8:30,31,34; Acts 14:14; Acts 21:40; Hosea 5:1.

12. **Temporary placing of the Divine Mind**: This is next done by the Spirit of truth **placing Faith and Love** in the mind **temporarily** that the person can now see the truth. Psalm 36:9; Daniel 3:28; Hosea 11:4; John 6:40-44.

13. **Conviction**: The next thing is that the person is **convicted** or **convinced** of sin, righteousness and judgement, to be able to now respond to God. Acts 2:37; Titus 1:9; John 16:8; Acts 16:29, 30.

14. The next point is **man's response** to **conviction**. He must **repent** which is to change his mind about the Carnal Mind's **values** and **idols**, these he must **reject**. Ezekiel 14:6; Luke 24:47; Revelation 3:19.

15. He must also at the same time **believe** the Gospel or Divine Mind of truth (Faith and Love). This believing is a mental acceptance of Faith with the **aim of being changed**. Genesis 15:6; Mark 1:14,15; John 3:15,16; Acts 13:39; Acts 16:25-34.

16. **Confession** is man **mentally** and **audibly** agreeing with God and

testifying that He is right, while the man requests change from God. All this is **confession**. Acts 8:37; Psalm 51:4; Romans 10:10.

17.   **Repentance** and **believing** is also **mental confession**. 1 John 1:9; Matthew 3:5-11; Psalm 32:5.

18.   Thus **Prevenient Grace** is the Grace of God **in the heart** of the **sinner before** he is converted; in order to evoke the response God desires that He may change the man. Acts 26:1-28.

19.   Under it, man may **repent, believe** and **confess** his sins **before** being **converted**. (Mark 1:14,15; Acts 13:39).

20.   The **glory of God** which is a **consuming fire** will slay the man **in whom Grace is** while he **has sin**, this is why Prevenient Grace is necessary. (Hebrews 12:29; Zechariah 14:12).

Renewing Grace (Justification)

1. This is the **change center** of the Plan of Salvation. It is so because this is the point where man is changed from **sinning** to **obedience**.

    a. After Repentance and Believing (Confession), the person is **justified**. (Mark 1:14,15; Acts 13:39).

2. There is indeed **Grace** that **renews** the repentant person. Titus 2:11-14; Titus 3:5-7.

3. This Grace is called the **Grace of Justification** or **Justification by Grace**. Romans 3:24.

4. The fact that Justification **changes** a person from **sinning** to **obedience** is seen in the fact that we **cease** to do wrong after we receive it. 1 Corinthians 6:9-11.

5. Justification is **Conversion** because once the person receives it, he is converted from **sinning** to **obedience** to God's Law. (1

Corinthians 6:9-11; Romans 3:30,31).

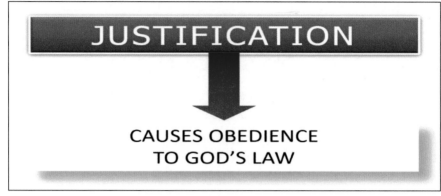

Figure (1) is a diagram on Justification and Obedience.

6.   Justification has two parts in its structure. They are:

   a.   The **non-imputation** of the sins of the carnal mind. Romans 4:8; 2 Corinthians 5:19.

   b.   The **imputation** of the Divine Mind or the Righteousness of God. (Romans 4:6; Romans 8:6; Romans 5:1).

See the following illustrative chart.

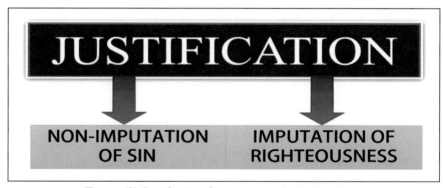

Figure (2) Justification has two parts in its structure.

7.   Justification has **two** basic **directions**, one from **God** and one towards **man**. They are:

   a.   The **God Action Direction** (GAD), which means that it is an act done by **God**, because, it is **God alone** that justifies. Romans 8:33; Romans 3:30.

b.   The **Man Transformative Direction** (MTD); this means that man is **transformed** from God's action of justifying him. Titus 3:5-7.

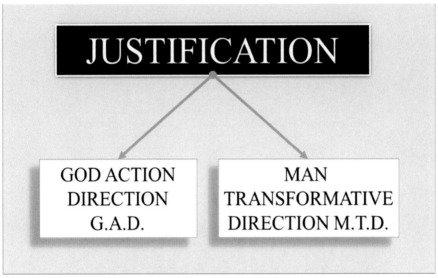

Figure (3) A diagram of the two basic directions of Justification.

8.   Because Justification **transforms** the man, we say that Justification is **subjective**, i.e. "subjective (inner) justification". 1 Corinthians 6:9-11. (Romans 12:2; Ezekiel 36:25-27). (Titus 3:5-7; Ephesians 2:2).

9.   Because Justification **changes the person**, we say that to be justified is to be "made righteous". (1 Corinthians 6:9-11; Romans 3:22; Romans 4:11).

See the following illustrative chart.

Figure (4) A diagram of what it means to be Justified.

10.   Justification is NEVER by **any** type of human works **ever**. Romans 4:1,2; Romans 9:31,32.

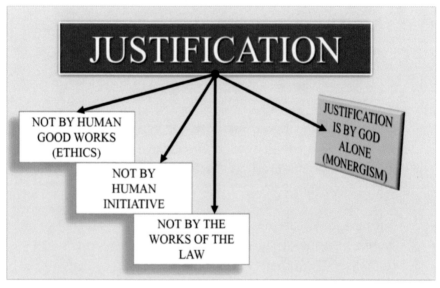

Figure (5) A diagram of the Monergism of Justification.

11.   Justification makes the person who receives it **sinfree**, that is, Justification makes him **cease** from **sinning**. Romans 6:1,2,6,7,18,22.

See the following illustrative chart.

Figure (6) A diagram of Justification and Sinfreeness.

12. Justification is **two transacted men** (T.T.M.). They are:

a. It is the **death** or removal of the **old man**. Romans 6:6,7.

b. It is the **gift** of the **new man**. (Ephesians 4:22-24; Colossians 3:9,10).

The chart below illustrates this fact.

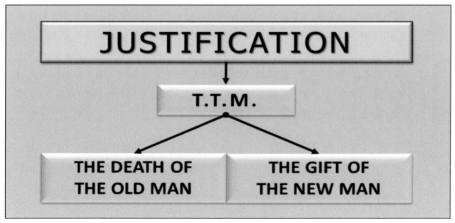

Figure (7) A diagram of Justification and its relation to the Old-man and the New-man.

13. Justification is also called the **new birth** or to be **born again**. (John 3:3,5-8; Galatians 3:6-9,14; Galatians 4:6).

14. Justification is the **removal** of the **carnal mind** and the **gift** of the **spiritual mind**. (Romans 8:6; Romans 5:1,18).

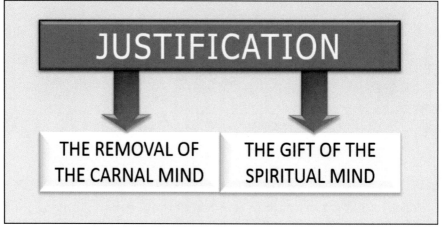

Figure (8) A diagram of Justification and its relation to the Carnal mind and the Spiritual mind.

15. Justification **first** deals with **sins in** the **mind**; that is, **idol values**. We are to **repent** of them because they **separate** or **alienate** us from God. (Ezekiel 14:5,6; Ezekiel 36:25-27; Isaiah 53:11).

16. Justification is the **gift** of the **Holy Spirit in the mind**, so that God may thereby dwell in the heart/mind. (Galatians 3:6-9,14; Galatians 4:6; 1 John 4:13).

The following chart (figure 9) on page 37 illustrates.

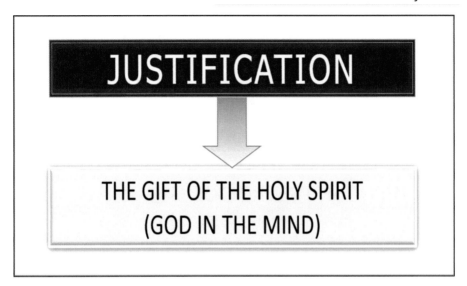

Figure (9) A diagram of Justification and the gift of the Holy Spirit.

17. Justification gives to the person his **new born again self**, which is portions of the **Character of Christ** dwelling in the person. (Romans 3:24,22; Ephesians 3:17; 2 Corinthians 4:6,7).

18. Justification is by the **Faith of Jesus Christ**, not by **human believing**. Galatians 2:16.

19. We must repent and **believe** the **Faith of Jesus Christ** (the Gospel) that we may be justified by the **Faith of Christ**. (Mark 1:14,15; Galatians 2:16).

20. Justification gives the **Righteousness of God** (God Himself) to dwell in us who **believe**. This is done by the **Faith of Jesus**. (Romans 3:24,22; Jeremiah 23:5,6).

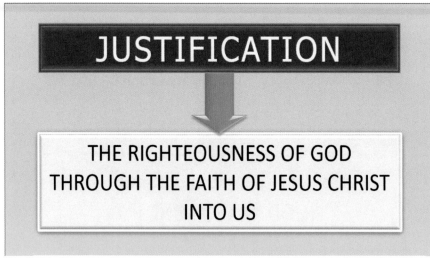

Figure (10) A diagram of Justification and the Righteousness of God.

21. Justification is done by God's **imputation**; this is a **mental estimation** from Him (not by a declaration). Romans 4:5,6,3.

22. To **impute** means to **really give**, but by the **esteeming** of the **mind**. Romans 4:9-11,3.

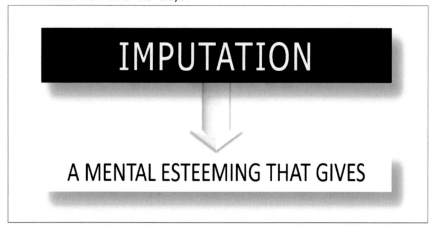

Figure (11) A diagram on the nature of Imputation.

23. A church stands or fall on the basis of **what is believed** concerning **Justification**. (Daniel 11:34; Isaiah 50:8,9).

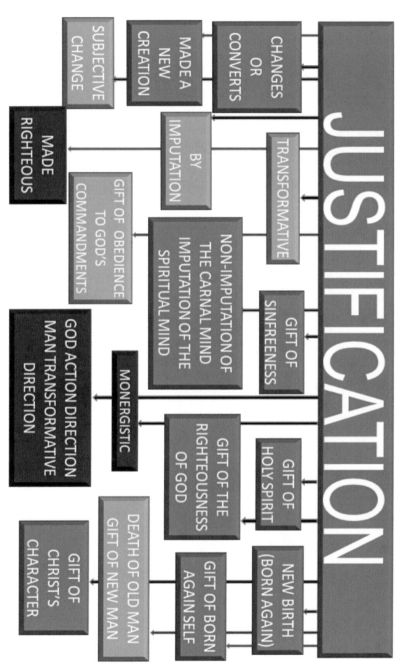

Figure (12) A diagram on all Justification means.

24.   Finally, Justification is to be made a **new creation**. (Romans 6:6, 7; Colossians 3:9,10).

25.   Since Justification is thus God's **recreative act** to penitent sinners, its symbol of this **new creation** is the **seventh day Sabbath**. (Romans 6:6,7; Colossians 3:9,10; 2 Corinthians 5:17; Exodus 31:16,17).

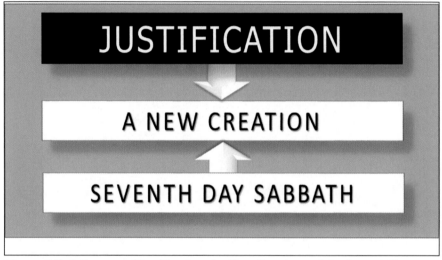

Figure (13) A diagram of Justification, the New Creation and the Seventh Day Sabbath.

PILLAR 6

Imparted Grace (Sanctification)

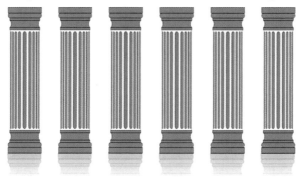

1. When we are **justified** we need to have it **maintained** in us, we need the continual **impartation** of the Grace of God or the doctrines of Grace. This is **Sanctification**. Acts 20:32; Acts 26:18.

2. **Sanctification** is **synergistic**; this means that both **God** and **man** are responsible for it. Philippians 2:12,13.

    a. God **imparts** the Faith to man. Romans 12:3; Ephesians 6:23.

    b. Man lives the Faith (or lives by Faith). Hebrews 10:36-39.

3. Sanctification is living **sinfree** in obedience to the **Law of God**. (Psalm 119:1-4; 1 Peter 1:2).

4. Sanctification is growth in the following:

a. The development of the **Character of Christ** by the reception of truth. (Galatians 4:19; 2 Peter 3:18).

b. The use of truth to develop **good human personality traits**. (Ephesians 4:32; 1 Peter 1:22).

5. In **Sanctification** we learn to maintain the following:

a. We maintain the Love of God in the heart. 1 John 3:11,14-19; 1 John 4:12.

b. We maintain obedience to the Law of God. 1 John 3:22-24; 1 John 5:1-4.

c. We maintain sinfreeness. 1 John 5:18; Psalm 119:9,11.

The following chart illustrates this reality.

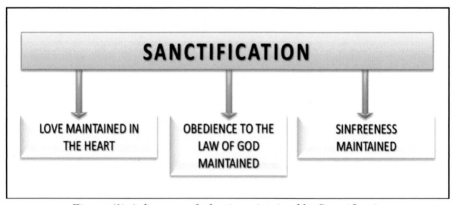

Figure (1) A diagram of what is maintained by Sanctification.

6. In Sanctification we learn to deal with the following:

a. We learn to handle **temptation to sin** by keeping it out of the life. Mark 14:38; 1 Corinthians 10:13; James 1:12.

b. We learn to handle the **infirmities** of our sinful flesh not allowing them to cause us to sin. Hebrews 4:14-16.

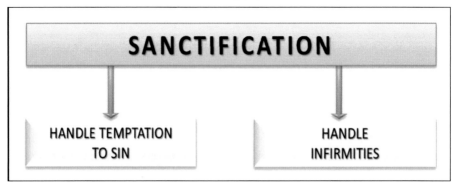

Figure (2) A diagram of Sanctification, Temptation and the Infirmities.

7. Sanctification is **eternal** in its operation; it is the work of a **lifetime**, because we will be **forever growing** in the Graces of **Christ's Character**. (John 14:6; 2 Peter 3:18).

8. Sanctification is within the orbit of sinfreeness (because, to fall into sin is to need justification again). Jude 1,24.

9. Most Christians experience what is called **Punctuated Sinfreeness**, that is, **sinfreeness sometimes** and **sinning sometimes** therefore needing Justification again. 1 John 2:1.

10. But the **ideal** from conversion is **All-Times Sinfreeness**; this is what we are to work towards. 1 John 3:9; Psalm 106:3.

11. Sanctification is made up of the following experiences:

    a. Lingering Victory.

    b. Conquering Victory.

    c. Achieved Victory.

    d. Sealed Perfection.

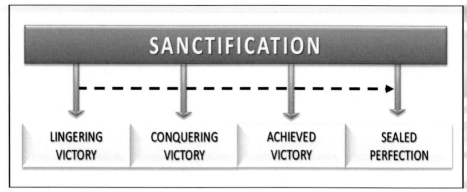

Figure (3) A diagram of the various experiences under Sanctification.

12. **Lingering Victory** is **sinfreeness maintained** by **lingering** or **abiding** in the truths or Faith of Christ. 1 John 3:6; John. 15:4,5.

13. **Conquering Victory** is **sinfreeness maintained** by also **conquering** the **sinful values** we once did, but are not doing as we are in Christ. Romans 8:35-39; 1 John 5:4,5,10-12; Ephesians 6:11,13-18.

14. **Achieved Victory** is victory over the sins peculiar to us as different persons; this is when we learn to have **All-Times Sinfreeness**. Psalm 119:44; 2 Timothy 4:7,8.

15. **Sealed Perfection** is when we are **sealed** in the state of **All-Times Sinfree Perfection** with the **Latter Rain** of the Holy Spirit so that we do not fall back into sin again. (Ephesians 4:30; Psalm 119:1-3; Revelation 14:1,4,5).

16. Sanctification is called **Justification by Works**. This is not **human initiative works**, it is works caused by **God working in man**. (Philippians 2:12,13; James 2:20-22).

The chart below illustrates this fact.

Figure (4) A diagram of Sanctification and Justification by works.

17.   This **Justification by works** is basically this:

    a.   We do works **inspired** by Faith. James 2:20,26.

    b.   Our good works show that we are **righteous** because the **glory of God** is seen in them. (James 2:22-24; Matthew 5:16).

18.   Sanctification is **Justification continued**, but without falling back into sin again and thus being recovered. It is God **esteeming** us righteous by virtue of the fact that we **do good works** from the Faith He gave to us. This is justification by works. (Hebrews 11:4; James 2:22-24).

Judicial Grace
(Investigative Judgment &
the Blotting out)

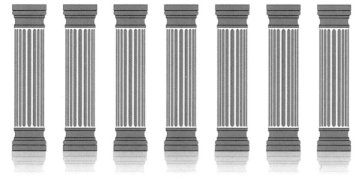

1. **Judgment** and **mercy** (Grace) do go together for salvational purposes. Psalm 101:1; Hosea 2:19; Hosea 12:6; Zechariah 7:9.

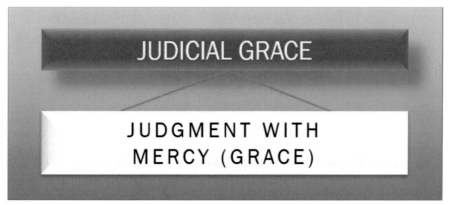

Figure (1) is a diagram on Judicial Grace.

2.   The concept of an **Investigative Judgment** and one done by **God** is truly Biblical. Revelation 20:12; Daniel 7:9,10.

3.   The concept of the **Blotting Out** of sins that are **past** is also Biblical. Psalm 109:14; Jeremiah 18:23.

4.   In the year **1844 A.C.B.** the **heavenly event** of the **cleansing of the sanctuary** beginning was revealed to **Adventism**.

    a.   On the **10th day** of the **seventh month**, the Israelites were given the symbolic festival of the **Day of Atonement**. Leviticus 23:27,28.

    b.   This service was called the **cleansing of the sanctuary**. Leviticus 16:19-21; Daniel 8:14.

    c.   The cleansing of the sanctuary was not the sanctuary itself being cleansed from some form of pollution that was actually defiling the sanctuary/tabernacle; it was a **cleansing work** of the sanctuary seen in the work of the **high priest** sprinkling the blood before the **mercy seat** of the second apartment, and on the curtain that divided the **first** and **second apartments**, (the "tabernacle of the congregation" and the "holy place"). Leviticus 16:2,3,14-17.

    d.   The **cleansing work** was also seen in the sins of Israel being placed upon the head of the **Scapegoat** at which he was sent away in the **wilderness** to die. This was Israel being cleansed from their **past sins**. Leviticus 16:20-22,29,30,34.

    e.   Observe the Charts on the following page.

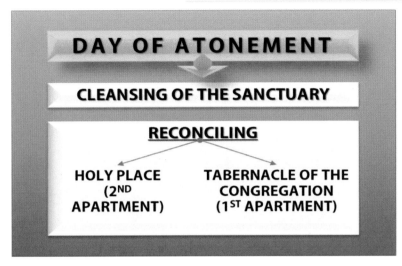

Figure (2) is a diagram on the Day of Atonement.

FIRST APARTMENT CALLED "TABERNACLE OF THE CONGREGATION"	SECOND APARTMENT CALLED "HOLY PLACE"
HOLY PLACE	MOST HOLY PLACE

Figure (3) is a diagram of the First and Second Apartments of the Sanctuary.

Figure (4) is a diagram on Cleansing of the Sanctuary.

f. This **cleansing of the sanctuary** was also called a
    Judgment (thus it is a judgment on the **Day of
    Atonement**). (Daniel 8:14; Daniel 7:9,10,22,26);
    Leviticus 23:27,28.

Figure (5) A diagram of the Cleansing of the Sanctuary and the Judgment.

5. Since these major feasts of Israel pertaining to the acceptable
    year of the Lord had **literal fulfillments** in time and history, so
    also must the **Day of Atonement**.
    a. A **literal** Passover of Jesus dying on the 14th of the **first
        month**, like the symbolic Passover, did happen.
        Leviticus 23:5; 1 Corinthians 5:7.

    b. A **literal firstfruits** on the **16th** of the **first month** in
        Jesus' resurrection, like the waving of the **firstfruits** on
        the 16th of the first month, did indeed happen. Leviticus
        23:6,7,10,11; 1 Corinthians 15:20,21.

    c. **Pentecost** was also literally fulfilled when the new
        church received the **Holy Spirit** as the true **wave
        loaves**, hence a kind of **firstfruits** unto the Lord.
        Leviticus 23:15-17,20; Acts 2:1-4,37-42; James 1:18.

d.   The **feast of trumpets** was on the **1st of the seventh month**. This was literally fulfilled in the **Millerite movement's** call to repentance because of the Judgment that was coming in **1844**, which is the **seventh angel's trumpet** sounding. Leviticus 23:24,25; Psalm 81:3; Isaiah 58:1; Joel 2:1,15-17; Revelation 10:5-7.

e.   The **Day of Atonement** began literally on **22nd October 1844**. The date **22nd of October** corresponds to the **10th day of the seventh month** according to the **Karaite Jews** reckoning. Leviticus 23:27,31; (Revelation 10:7; Revelation 11:15-19).

f.   The **Feast of tabernacles** is yet future to be fulfilled. Leviticus 23:34-36.

PASSOVER 14TH, 1st mth.	**JESUS' DEATH** 14TH, 1st mth.
FIRST FRUITS 16TH, 1st mth.	**JESUS' RESURRECTION** 16TH, 1st mth.
PENTECOST 50 DAYS AFTER 16th, 1st mth.	**CHURCH SETUP** **31 A.C.B.** 50 DAYS AFTER 16TH, 1st mth.
FEAST OF TRUMPETS 1ST, 7TH mth.	**MILLERITE WARNINGS** 1833 – 1843 A.C.B.
DAY OF ATONEMENT 10TH, 7TH mth.	**JUDGMENT IN HEAVEN** 22ND OCTOBER 1844
FEAST OF TABERNACLES 15TH - 21st , 7TH mth.	**?** **(FUTURE)**

Figure (6) A diagram of the Feasts and their Fulfillments in time and History.

6. The **Day of Atonement** was literally fulfilled on the 22nd October, in the year **1844 A.C.B.**

   a. **The 2300 days** equal years, at the end of which the cleansing work of the **sanctuary in heaven** was to begin. Daniel 8:14,17,19,26; (Numbers 14:34).

   b. This date starts from the going forth of the commandment to restore and rebuild Jerusalem which was given, then executed from the fifth month (July-August according to Jewish reckoning) of the **seventh year** of King **Artaxerxes Longimanus**, which was 457 B.C.B. (Daniel 9:25; Ezra 7:1,6-9,11-13).

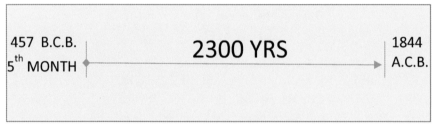

Figure (7) is a diagram on the 2300 Years.

   c. There is actually a real **heavenly sanctuary** from which the type on earth was made. Hebrews 8:1,2,5; Hebrews 9:11; Revelation 11:19.

   d. That the heavenly Sanctuary also needed **cleansing** is seen. Hebrews 9:23.

   e. The following Scripture shows us when the cleansing work of the heavenly sanctuary, the **Investigative Judgment** and **Blotting Out** of past sins, actually began. Revelation 11:18,19.

   f. The cleansing work of the heavenly sanctuary occurs in the second apartment where the ark of the testimony (the Law) was seen. This takes place in the Most Holy

Place. (Revelation 11:19; Deuteronomy 10:1-5; Exodus 31:18; Psalm 78:5,7).

FIRST APARTMENT	SECOND APARTMENT
"TABERNACLE OF THE CONGREGATION" "TA HAGIA" (THE HOLIES)	"HOLY PLACE" "HAGIA HAGION" HOLIES HOLIES ARK WITH THE LAW
HOLY PLACE	MOST HOLY PLACE

CLEANSING OF THE SANCTUARY

INVESTIGATIVE JUDGMENT, BLOTTING OUT OCCURS HERE

Figure (8) is a diagram on the Cleansing Work in the 2nd Apartment of the Heavenly Sanctuary.

g.   The **first apartment** of the heavenly sanctuary in Hebrews is called "Ta Hagia" or "the holies". Hebrews 9:1,2; (See also: Hebrews 9:12,24; Hebrews 10:19).

h.   The **second apartment** of the heavenly sanctuary in Hebrews is called "Hagia Hagion" in the Greek. It means "holies holies". Hebrews 9:3.

7.   **Justification** is **forgiveness of sins**. Romans 4:5-8; Acts 13:38, 39.

8.   Since **this Judgment is justification**, then it is also the **forgiveness of sins**. Matthew 12:36,37.

Figure (9) is a diagram on Justification, Forgiveness of Sins and Judgment.

9.   There are **three justifications**. They are:

    a.   Justification by **Faith/Grace** (Renewal). Titus 3:5-7.

    b.   Justification by **Works** (Sanctification). James 2:20-24.

    c.   Justification on the **account of works** (the Blotting Out of sins). (Romans 2:13; Psalm 119:166).

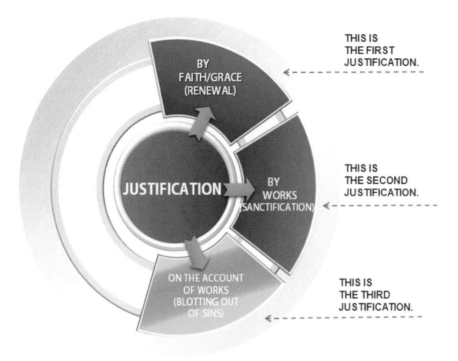

Figure (10) is a diagram on the Three Justifications.

10. Since the **blotting out of sins** occurs only **after conversion** (which means the person is changed already), then it cannot be for sins that are alive within the person (sinning), it has to be for **past sins**. Acts 3:19.

11. Since the **blotting out of sins** is for **past sins**, and **Justification** is also for **past sins**, then it follows, that the **blotting out** of past sins is Justification and is also **forgiveness of sins that are past**. Acts 3:19; Acts 13:38,39; Romans 2:16. See Figure (11) chart below.

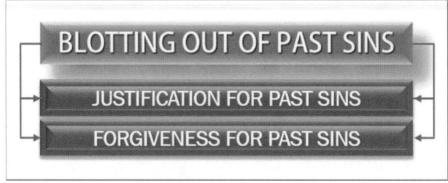

Figure (11) Blotting out of Past Sins is Justification and Forgiveness for past sins.

12. We are all condemned for two things when we are converted. They are:

a. Sins within or present sinning. Genesis 6:5-7; Romans 8:6-8; Titus 3:11.

b. **Past sins** that have already been committed. Matthews 27:3; 2 Peters 2:16.

13. We escape **condemnation first** for the **sins within**, because they have been **removed first** by God and the Character of Christ and God has taken their places. Matthew 23:25,26; Romans 8:1-4.

14. We escape **condemnation** for **past sins** when we are **converted** in **obedience** to God. James 5:19,20; 1 John 4:16,17; 1 Peter 4:8.

15. Sins basically have **four categories**.

a. Past-Present sins

b. Present sinning.

c. Past sins.

d. Historical past sins.

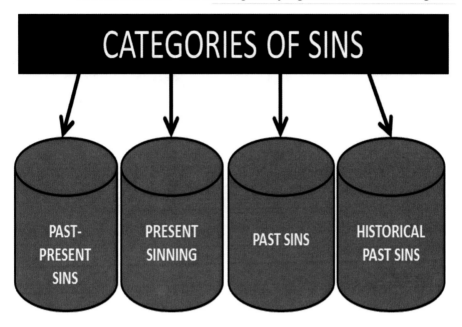

CATEGORIES OF SINS

| PAST-PRESENT SINS | PRESENT SINNING | PAST SINS | HISTORICAL PAST SINS |

Figure (12) is a diagram on Four Categories of Sins.

16.   **Past-Present sins** identify **the idol-values that are present** as the **carnal mind** but it was in the man always as the **past**. So to identify this type of sins we call it **past** (from the past existence of it), **Present** (from the fact that it is present in the heart of the unconverted as a value), **sins** (because the person is **sinning** by its presence and **was sinning** in the **past** by its presence in the person), hence the name **Past-Present Sins**. Ezekiel 8:10-12; Ezekiel 14:3,5.

17.   **Present sinning** is the **moral state** of the **unconverted person**; he is **in** his sins, or **is sinning**. He has the carnal mind in him and idol-values in his heart. He **is in the act of committing the sin**. Romans 8:6-8; Ezekiel 14:4,5; Matthew 26:69-74.

18.   **Past sins** are sins that have **just been committed**, and are **no longer** being committed at the moment. Matthew 27:3,4, Exodus 10:16; Psalm 51:4.

19. **Historical past sins** are sins we do **not ever commit again** because we have **gained the victory** over them. His **past sins** become **history** because he does them **no more**. These are the sins that are **blotted out** or **forgiven**. Psalm 119:9,1-3; Acts 3:19; James 5:20.

20. **Past sins** have **three categories**.
    a. The past sins of the **unconverted**.

    b. The past sins of the **converted**.

    c. Past sins **never again committed** (called Historical past sins).

21. An **unconverted person** may stop a **particular sin** thus making it a past sin, but, as he is not converted, he still goes on sinning in different ways. Nehemiah 13:16-22.

22. A **converted person**, when he became converted, has stopped the sins he was committing, making them become **past sins**, but he has not yet gained the victory over them, and may fall back into them needing Justification again. This is the past sins of the converted person. 1 John 2:1; 1 John 5:16,17.

23. But all the sins that the converted person **never commit again** because he has **overcome** them, and their committal means nothing to him of value, these sins are more **distant** from him, so we call them **historical past sins**. 1 John 4:16,17; 1 John 3:9; 2 Timothy 2:21,22; 2 Timothy 4:6-8.

24. Thus the **blotting out of sins** in the judgment is indeed **forgiveness** for **historical past** sins. (Acts 3:19; Romans 2:13,16).

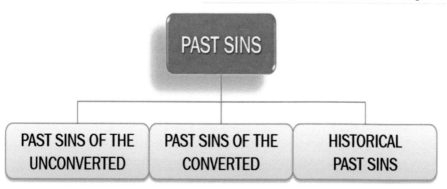

Figure (13) is a diagram on Three Categories of Past Sins.

25.　This blotting out of sins is called **forensic justification** because it is justification that occurs in the judgment hence in the heavenly courts (forum). Romans 2:13,16; Matthew 12:36, 37.

26.　This blotting out of past sins is also called a **declaration** that is **justification**; it is being **declared righteous** because a state of sinfree righteousness **already exists** in the person's life. Hence, the man only needs to be **declared righteous** when his **historical past sins** are being forgiven. (Daniel 7:22; Revelation 22:11,12).

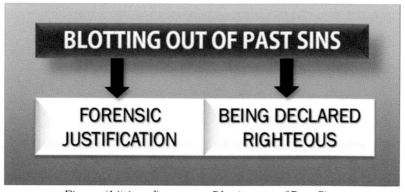

Figure (14) is a diagram on Blotting out of Past Sins.

27.　This all shows us that the **Investigative Judgement** or the **blotting out** is really **forgiveness** for **historical past sins**. (Romans 2:13,16; Acts 13:38,39).

28. Another part of this **Day of Atonement Judgment** is the sins of the saints being placed upon the head of the **scapegoat**. We call this the **Post-Redemptive Substantiatory**. Leviticus 16:20-22.

   a. This scapegoat is not a symbol of Christ because it never is slain for man's sins to get its blood, like the **first goat**; it is kept alive while atonement is made. However, with Jesus, where there is no shedding of blood, there is **no remission**. Hebrews 9:14,19-22.

   b. **Post-Redemptive Substantiatory** actually means a redemption that is **ratified** or **substantiated** even after it is accomplished already. It is like throwing the rubbish in a **bin** from the house that it was cleansed from. Throwing the rubbish in a bin is the same as cleansing the house even though it was already cleansed. This is what we call a **post-cleansing-substantiating** work; it is a work that substantiates the **cleansing** that has been completed. This is seen with regards to the scapegoat. Leviticus 16:8-10,15,16,18-22, 29,30.

29. The actual Hebrew word for "scapegoat" is "**Azazel**". The word is from "azaz" which means "fierce", "az" from "azaz", which means "goat", and "el" which means "god". Thus the word actually means "Fierce goat god". This, is what we today call "**Baphomet**" or "**Mendes**". Leviticus 16:8.

   a. The facts are; there were wild goats in the wilderness. Isaiah 13:19-22; Isaiah 34:13,14; (Luke 11:24).

   b. That **goats** were worshipped as **demons** in the desert, that were **gods**, is seen. Leviticus 17:7; 2 Kings 23:8; 2 Chronicles 11:15.

Figure (15) is a diagram on Azazel.

30. The past sins of the saved Christians, that have been **blotted out**, or that they were forgiven for, are placed upon Satan's head as the one responsible for them committing them. This happens during the 1000 years that Satan is bound to the earth, when the saints are in heaven judging the records of the wicked. Leviticus 16:20-22; Revelation 20:1-4.

31. The **lost wicked** will thus pay for their own sins in hell-fires although Satan caused them to commit them. But their guilt is that they never accepted Jesus' salvation to be freed from their condemnation. Matthew 25:41-46.

32. But Satan pays for his own sins, parts of which are the sins he caused the saints, who were eventually saved, to commit. This is the **Post-Redemptive Substantiatory** where Satan receives death as the **rebel** and **tempter**. Malachi 4:1; Ezekiel 28:18,19; Revelation 20:7,10.

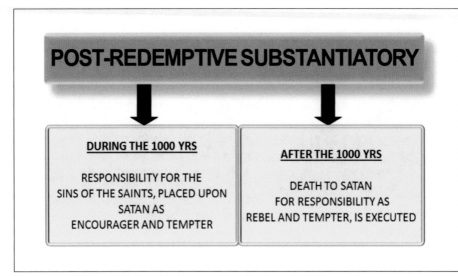

Figure (16) is a diagram on Post Redemptive Substantiatory.

33. In the **Investigative Judgment** three books/scrolls are used. They are:

    a. The book of iniquity.

    b. The book of remembrance.

    c. The book of life.

34. The **book of iniquity** contains all the sinful practices of all the wicked in the history of the world that ever sinned. Jeremiah 2:22.

35. The **book of remembrance** contains all the good deeds of the person from his **conversion** to his **death in Christ** and the good deeds of the 144,000 also. Malachi 3:16.

36. The **book of life** is a record of all the names of those who have accepted Christ's salvation. (Luke 10:20; Revelation 20:12).

37. It is **in** the Investigative Judgment that names are **removed** from the **book of life** or are **retained** therein. (Revelation 3:5; Revelation 20:12-15).

a. Those who died in Jesus and the 144,000 who were sealed, their names are **retained** in **the book of life** as all their past sins are forgiven (justified/blotted out). (Revelation 3:5; Mathew 10:32,33); Romans 2:13,16.

b. Those who **once** followed Christ but eventually **turned away** for whatever reasons, their names will be removed from the **book of life** as their sins are **retained**. Exodus 32:31-33.

c. The **book of remembrance** testifies why the names of the **converted, who remained converted**, are kept in the **book of life**. Malachi 3:16-18.

d. Any **good done** by those who were converted but then turned away from God, which are still written in the **book of remembrance**, will **not be mentioned** for his favor, since they were done only through Christ the vine, and he turned away from Him and died in his sins. (Exodus 32:31-33; Ezekiel 18:24).

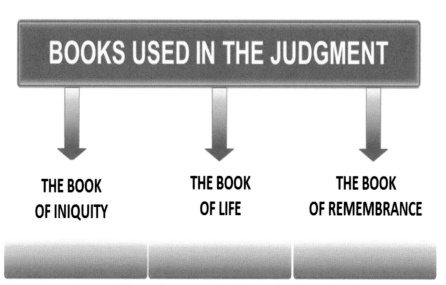

Figure (17) is a diagram on Books used in the Judgment.

38.   Here are other ways in which the Investigative Judgment and Blotting Out are presented in the Bible.

    a.   The sins and iniquities of the righteous will not be remembered by God in the Judgment. Hebrews 8:10-12, Hebrews 10:16-18.

    b.   We must be **found** in Christ's Righteousness (in the Judgment). Philippians 3:8-10.

    c.   "For we through Spirit, out of faith, **hope of righteousness** we are eagerly awaiting" (in the Judgment). Galatians 5:5.

    d.   Only Faith which works by Love (in it) avails us (in the Judgment). Galatians 5:6.

    e.   Those with Christ during the **year of the plagues**, after probation is closed, are **chosen** (in the Judgment). Revelation 17:14.

    f.   We must be found with a **wedding garment** of **Righteousness** in the wedding when we are **investigated** by the king in the Judgment. Matthew 22:1-14.

    g.   We are **heirs** of the kingdom as converted people, but we will only **inherit** the kingdom in the **Judgment**, causing the subjects of the kingdom to be made up. (James 2:5; Matthew 25:34; Daniel 2:44).

    h.   The great Prince **standeth** for the children of thy people in the **Judgment**, but when He stands up (the Judgment finishes) then the **year of the plagues** or **time of trouble** begins. (Daniel 12:1; Isaiah 3:13).

39. The Investigative Judgment and Blotting Out as an event beginning in 1844 A.C.B. is comparable to the death of Christ on the Cross in 31 A.C.B.

SYSTEMATIC THEOLOGY
(1986 Edition)

The following picture book is the **original Systematic Theology** *that was* **first published in the year 1986** *by Bro.* **Nyron Medina, founding Minister** *of the* **Thusia Seventh day Adventist Church**-*the* **independent Revival of original Seventh day Adventism** *and* **Ancient Apostolic Christianity.** *It was handwritten and drawn by Bro. Nyron Medina using comic booklet style for effect, to convey the* **light of truths revealed by God to him** *in the early years of the existence of this* **reformation movement.**

This copy remains with **detailed explanations** *and a* **wide variety of textual ratifications** *on the Seven Pillars of Systematic Theology, and it is the* **Author's intention** *that the* **reader studies it in conjunction with** *the more recent book, for* **full understanding of the revelations** *which constitute the* **Whole Great Grand Atonement (the Plan of Salvation)** *that is the* **Systematic Theology.**

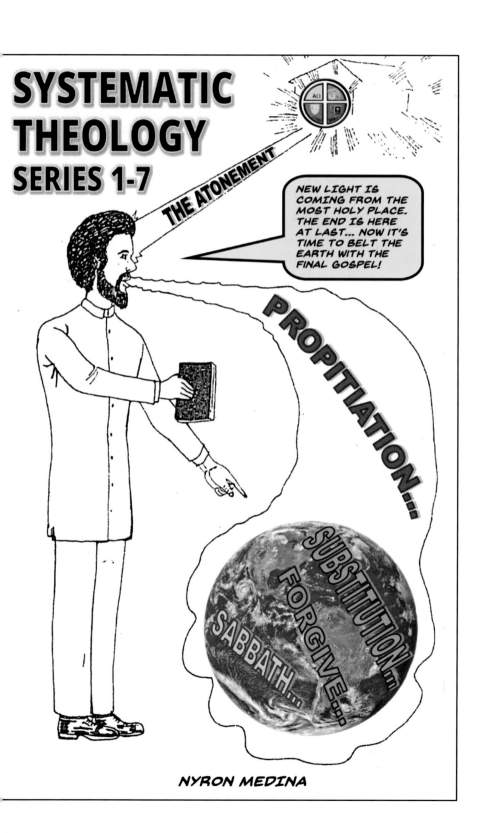

A COURSE IN SYSTEMATIC THEOLOGY

BY NYRON MEDINA

PILLAR ONE: — THE GODHEAD

IT IS TRUE THAT GOD EXISTED BEFORE ALL THINGS (JOHN 1:3; COLOSSIANS 1:16,17). GOD IS THE **PRETHESIS** (FIRST KNOWLEDGE), AND WHEN HE BEGINS TO CREATE, THE KNOWLEDGE OF HIS CREATION COMES FROM HIM, THUS THE KNOWLWDGE OF HIS CREATION IS THE **SUBTHESIS** (OR SECOND KNOWLEDGE) SUBJECTED TO WHAT GOD IS. IN THE SUBTHESIS, CREATION MUST BE SEEN, IN CONTEXT TO GOD, AND NOT GOD IN CONTEXT TO CREATION.

THE MISTAKE WITH FALSE THEOLOGY IS THAT GOD IS NOT KNOWN. THEY START OFF WITH A FALSE VIEW OF GOD WHICH COLOURS THEIR THEOLOGY, CHRISTOLOGY, SOTERIOLOGY, ANTHROPOLOGY, HARMATOLOGY, PNEUMATOLOGY AND ESCHATOLOGY!

FOR EXAMPLE, A LACK OF UNDERSTANDING OF THE REAL TRUE NATURE OF GOD WILL EFFECT AN ANTHROPOLOGICAL DOCTRINE TO THE EFFECT OF TEACHING THAT MAN HAS AN IMMORTAL SOUL (WHICH IS REALLY SAYING THAT HE HAS INHERENT ETERNAL LIFE). OR WE MIGHT VIEW SIN AS A TYPE OF FLESH IN OUR HARMATOLOGY DETERMINING OUR CHRISTOLOGY AND SOTERIOLOGY, IF WE DO NOT UNDERSTAND WHAT IS **RIGHTEOUSNESS** AS THE NATURE OF GOD. THUS GOD MUST BE VIEWED AS THE 'A PRIORI' IN RETROSPECT TO CREATION THAT EACH MAY HAVE ITS DISTINCT IMAGE IN OUR MINDS TO AN ACCURATE UNDERSTANDING OF SIN AND GOD'S MEANS TO DEAL WITH IT!

TO BE FREE FROM ERRORS WITH REGARDS TO THE WHOLE ISSUE OF SALVATION, WE MUST FIRST UNDERSTAND GOD AS HE IS REVEALED IN THE **SPIRITUAL LAW**, AND ALL THINGS ELSE IN CONTEXT TO THIS! THIS IS WHY **SYSTEMATIC THEOLOGY** MUST FIRST BEGIN WITH THE KNOWLEDGE OF GOD AS HE IS REVEALED IN THE **THREE PERSONS-OFFICES**, AND OF HIS DIVINE NATURE AS IS REVEALED IN THE **SPIRITUAL LAW**!

THE CONCLUSIONS DERIVED FROM THE ABOVE STUDY ARE THESE:

(A.) GOD IS **NOT** A SHAPE OR FORM. HE IS SHAPELESS OR FORMLESS. GOD IS **INVISIBLE** OR **UNSEEN**, GOD IS **SPIRIT!**

(B.) GOD IS **ONE**, NOT TWO OR THREE, BUT HE IS MANIFESTED IN **THREE PERSONS-OFFICES** COMMONLY CALLED **THE FATHER, SON AND SPIRIT**. WE WOULD RATHER SAY **THE ANCIENT OF DAYS, THE WORD AND THE SPIRIT!**

(C.) GOD IS NOT KNOWN BY A PARTICULAR LOOK OR SHAPE, HE CANNOT BE SEEN, WE CAN ONLY KNOW HIM BY UNDERSTANDING THE STRUCTURE OF HIS NATURE WHICH IS THE **SPIRITUAL LAW**, AND THIS HE SUBSTANTIATES IN OUR MINDS BY PROGRESSIVE AND ETERNAL UNFOLDING OF THE TRUTHS OF THE GREAT, GRAND **ATONEMENT**.

(D.) TO KNOW GOD IS TO KNOW THE **SPIRITUAL LAW**.

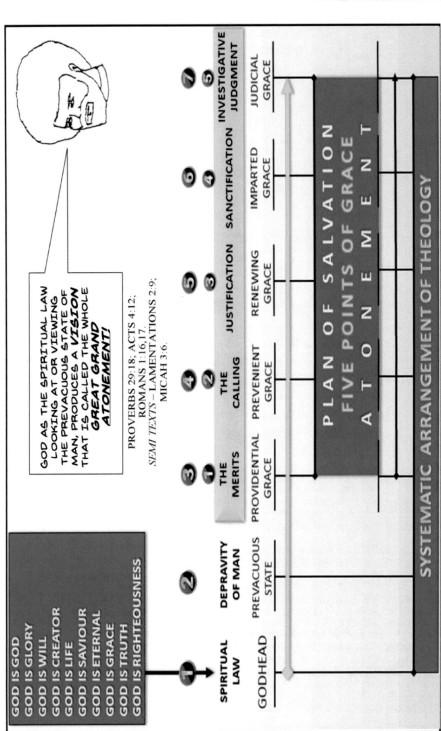

GOD IS GOD
GOD IS GLORY
GOD IS WILL
GOD IS CREATOR
GOD IS LIFE
GOD IS SAVIOUR
GOD IS ETERNAL
GOD IS GRACE
GOD IS TRUTH
GOD IS RIGHTEOUSNESS

GOD AS THE SPIRITUAL LAW LOOKING AT OR VIEWING THE PREVACUOUS STATE OF MAN, PRODUCES A *VISION* THAT IS CALLED THE WHOLE ***GREAT GRAND ATONEMENT!***

PROVERBS 29:18; ACTS 4:12; ROMANS 1:16,17.
SEMI TEXTS – LAMENTATIONS 2:9; MICAH 3:6.

GODHEAD		DEPRAVITY OF MAN		THE MERITS	THE CALLING	JUSTIFICATION	SANCTIFICATION	INVESTIGATIVE JUDGMENT
	SPIRITUAL LAW	PREVACUOUS STATE	PROVIDENTIAL GRACE	PREVENIENT GRACE	RENEWING GRACE	IMPARTED GRACE	JUDICIAL GRACE

PLAN OF SALVATION
FIVE POINTS OF GRACE
ATONEMENT

SYSTEMATIC ARRANGEMENT OF THEOLOGY

III

SYSTEMATIC THEOLOGY SERIES 1-7

THE PREVACUOUS STATE (DEPRAVITY OF MAN)

WHAT A DEPRAVED WORM IS MAN, WALLOWING IN THE MIRE AND FILTH OF THE EARTH...

CARNAL MIND, BODY OF SINS, EVIL WORKS...

NYRON MEDINA

A COURSE IN SYSTEMATIC THEOLOGY

BY NYRON MEDINA

PILLAR 2   DEPRAVITY OF MAN

THE REBELLION OF LUCIFER MADE IT NECESSARY FOR GOD TO CREATE MAN, WHO WOULD **GLORIFY** GOD TO NEGATE THE DECEPTIONS OF SATAN! IN THE BEGINNING MAN WAS MADE IN THE **IMAGE**, AFTER THE LIKENESS OF GOD! GENESIS 1:26,27.

TO BE MADE IN THE **IMAGE OF GOD** IS TO BE CREATED WITH THE DIVINE NATURE IN YOU! SEE: HEBREWS 1:3;2; CORINTHIANS 4:4; COLOSSIANS 1:15; PHILIPPIANS 2:6; (PSALM 25:8; ECCLESIASTES 7:29). THIS MEANS THAT MAN WAS CREATED SINFREE!

IT IS ONLY OBVIOUS THAT MAN HAS THE **SHAPE** AND **FORM** THAT THE PERSONS OF THE **FATHER** AND **SON** HAVE! MAN HAS HANDS, EYES, HEAD, MOUTH AND FEET ETC. LIKE FATHER AND SON POSSESS, BUT THIS IS NOT POSSESSING MORAL UPRIGHTNESS!

IN THE SIN OF **ADAM** AND **EVE** THE GENESIS OF THE DEPRAVITY OF MAN IS CLEARLY SEEN! IN MAN'S SIN, HE LOST THE **DIVINE NATURE** AND DEVELOPED **PERVERTED AFFECTIONS**. READ: GENESIS 3:1-6.

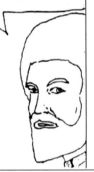

ADAM WAS AFRAID, GENESIS 3:10, PERFECT **LOVE** CASTS OUT ALL FEAR, 1 JOHN 4:12,16-18. THUS ADAM AND EVE LOST THE **LOVE OF GOD** OR THE **SPIRITUAL LAW**. THEY SINNED WHICH IS TRANSGRESSION OF THE LAW, 1 JOHN 3:4; JAMES 2:8,9. SEE ROMANS 3:23. SO THEY LOST THE **LOVE** OF GOD, THEY WERE **VACUOUS**, OR EMPTY OF GOD.

ADAM AND EVE DEVELOPED **SINFUL FLESH**, THAT IS, THEIR FLESH WAS NOW **LIABLE** OF HAVING PERVERTED EMOTIONS FLOWING IN IT, AND IT HAD **INFIRMITIES**. THIS IS NOT SIN THIS IS THE **EFFECT** OF SIN UPON THE FLESH! ALL ADAM'S DESCENDANTS INHERIT THIS FLESH, INCLUDING CHRIST. BUT WITHOUT CHRIST IN THE HEART KEEPING THE FLESH IN SUBJECTION, THE **LIABILITIES** BECOME THE ACTUAL FLOW OF PERVERTED EMOTIONS OR THE BODY OF SINS, AND THE **INFIRMITIES** LEAD TO SIN!

THIS NEVER HAPPENED TO JESUS CHRIST, BECAUSE HIS SINFUL FLESH WAS ALWAYS SUBJECTED TO DEITY!

ADAM AND EVE GAVE TO THEIR DESCENDANTS THE **SINFUL FLESH**, AND AS THEY ARE CONCEIVED WITHOUT GOD FROM THE WOMB, THEY DEVELOP THE **CARNAL MIND** IN A PRIMITIVE FORM, AND PERVERTED FEELINGS FLOW! SO NOT ONLY THROUGH **BIOLOGICAL INHERITANCE**, BUT ALSO THROUGH **INFLUENCIVE INHERITANCE** MEN ARE MADE SINNERS AS THEY HAVE NOT GOD IN THEM TO HOLD BACK SIN!

READ THESE TEXTS: ROMANS 5:12,15,19; EXODUS 20:5; EXODUS 34:7; JOB 15:16; PSALM 14:3. ISAIAH 1:6; ISAIAH 59:2,3; PSALM 51:5; PSALM 58:3; ISAIAH 48:8; ISAIAH 64:6; MATTHEW 23:27,28,33; ROMANS 1:24,29-31; ROMANS 3:12-18; 1 TIMOTHY 1:9,10; EPHESIANS 4:22. THEY ALL EMPHASIZE THE DEPRAVITY OF MAN!

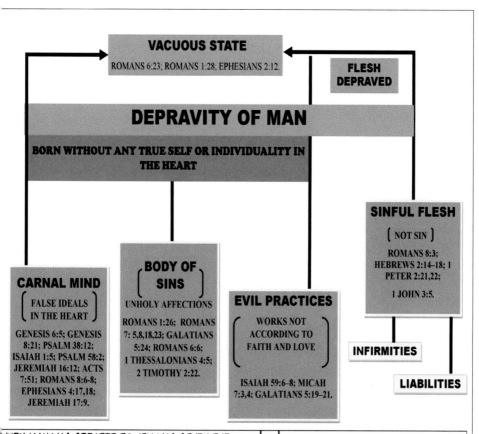

VACUOUS STATE
ROMANS 6:23; ROMANS 1:28; EPHESIANS 2:12.

FLESH DEPRAVED

DEPRAVITY OF MAN

BORN WITHOUT ANY TRUE SELF OR INDIVIDUALITY IN THE HEART

SINFUL FLESH

(NOT SIN)

ROMANS 8:3; HEBREWS 2:14–18; 1 PETER 2:21,22;

1 JOHN 3:5.

CARNAL MIND

[FALSE IDEALS IN THE HEART]

GENESIS 6:5; GENESIS 8:21; PSALM 38:12; ISAIAH 1:5; PSALM 58:2; JEREMIAH 16:12; ACTS 7:51; ROMANS 8:6-8; EPHESIANS 4:17,18; JEREMIAH 17:9.

BODY OF SINS

UNHOLY AFFECTIONS

ROMANS 1:26; ROMANS 7: 5,8,18,23; GALATIANS 5:24; ROMANS 6:6; 1 THESSALONIANS 4:5; 2 TIMOTHY 2:22.

EVIL PRACTICES

[WORKS NOT ACCORDING TO FAITH AND LOVE]

ISAIAH 59:6–8; MICAH 7:3,4; GALATIANS 5:19–21.

INFIRMITIES

LIABILITIES

WHEN MAN WAS CREATED TO HIM WAS GIVEN THE *PLAN OF DOMINION* (GENESIS 1: 26) IN WHICH WAS HIS TRUE SELF OR INDIVIDUALITY AND THOSE OF ALL OF HIS DESCENDANTS! WHEN MAN SINNED HE REJECTED THE PLAN AND NOW HAD THE *CARNAL MIND* AND THE *BODY OF SINS*. THE EARTH WAS NOW DAMAGED AND AS SATAN WOULD HAVE CONTROL OVER THE DESCENDANTS OF ADAM, MAN COULD NOT HAVE DOMINION AGAIN. SO GOD HAD TO DISPENSE WITH THE *PLAN OF DOMINION*, AND WITH IT THE TRUE SELVES OR INDIVIDUALITIES OF ADAM AND ALL OF HIS DESCENDANTS, THUS ALL MEN ARE BORN UNCONVERTED AND LOST WITHOUT GOD! GOD MUST FIRST CONVINCE THEM OF HIS LOVE IN THE NEW PLAN (*THE ATONEMENT*) THAT HE HAS INSTITUTED TO RECONCILE MEN TO HIMSELF.

SO THE *DEPRAVITY OF MAN* IS THAT MAN IS BORN WITHOUT INHERENT RIGHTEOUSNESS, BORN WITH THE CARNAL MIND, DEVELOPING THE BODY OF SINS! THIS IS WHAT THE ATONEMENT WAS INSTITUTED TO CORRECT, THIS ALSO TAKES INTO ACCOUNT MAN'S GUILT FOR PAST SINS!

WE DO NOT SUBSCRIBE TO AGUSTINIAN *"ORIGINAL SIN"*. THIS TERM IS A CONCEPT THAT MIXES THE SINFUL FLESH TOGETHER WITH THE FLOWING PERVERTED EMOTIONS, AND IT HAS CAUSED CONFUSION WITH REGARDS TO CHRISTOLOGY AND SOTERIOLOGY!

THE TRUE CONCEPTS WE HAVE HERE PRESENTED CAN REVEAL OUR CHRISTOLOGY AND SOTERIOLOGY. IT IS THIS THAT MAKES US WHAT WE ARE, WE ARE THUSIAN ADVENTISTS, AND THROUGH THE TRUTH WE SHALL OVERCOME SIN AND BRING CHRIST BACK TO THE EARTH IN OUR GENERATION!

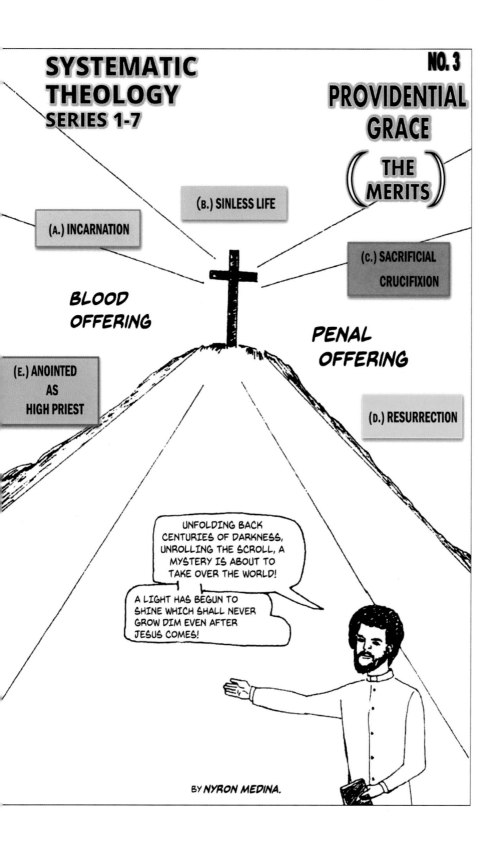

A COURSE IN SYSTEMATIC THEOLOGY

BY NYRON MEDINA

PILLAR THREE: PROVIDENTIAL GRACE (THE MERITS)

BECAUSE GOD IS **ONE SPIRITUAL NATURE** THAT DWELLS IN THREE PERSONS-OFFICES, BECAUSE THAT SPIRITUAL NATURE IS **LOVE**, THAT SAME LOVE LOOKING AT THE **PREVACUOUS STATE**, OR VIEWING THE **DEPRAVITY OF MAN**, PRODUCES A VISION CALLED THE GREAT GRAND **ATONEMENT**. THIS IS THE **WILL** OF GOD, THE **MEDIATIVE** WORK OF CHRIST OR THE ACTIVE, ENERGIZING, **CREATIVE** TRUTHS THAT THE HOLY SPIRIT IS, THAT GOD HAS INSTITUTED TO SAVE SINFUL MAN. IN THIS PLAN, GOD'S ONE NATURE OF LOVE IS HELD AND IS IMPARTED TO MAN THAT GOD MAY DWELL IN HIM, AND THIS CONSTITUTES SALVATION, THIS CONSTITUTES PERFECTION!

THE PLAN OF ATONEMENT STARTS OFF WITH **PROVIDENTIAL GRACE**. THIS FIRST COMPONENT IDENTIFIES THE **GRACE OF GOD** AS IT IS PROVIDED TO SAVE MAN! TAKING THE EFFECTIVE IMPUTATIVE CHANGE OF **JUSTIFICATION** AS THE OBJECTIVE, IN THE **FIVE POINTS OF GRACE** OR SYSTEMATIC JUSTIFICATION, PROVIDENTIAL GRACE IS THE **FOUNDATION** OF JUSTIFICATION AND IT IS FOLLOWED BY **PREVENIENT GRACE, RENEWING GRACE, IMPARTED GRACE** AND **JUDICIAL GRACE**!

THIS IS THE WHOLE, GREAT, GRAND ATONEMENT. THIS IS THE GOSPEL IN A SYSTEMATIC PATTERN. THIS IS THE FOUNDATION OF THE FAITH OF **SEVENTH-DAY ADVENTISTS** AS IS ENUNCIATED IN THE HOLY SCRIPTURES. THE FOLLOWING IS A SYSTEMATIC LAYOUT OF THE FIVE POINTS:

(1) THE FOUNDATIONS OF JUSTIFICATION:
PROVIDENTIAL GRACE

(2) THE CONDITIONS OF JUSTIFICATION:
PREVENIENT GRACE

(3) THE MEANS OF JUSTIFICATION:
RENEWING GRACE

(4) THE RESULTS OF JUSTIFICATION:
IMPARTED GRACE

(5) THE END OF JUSTIFICATION:
JUDICIAL GRACE

THERE MUST BE A GROUND OR FOUNDATION OF JUSTIFICATION. THERE MUST BE CONDITIONS, NOT ONLY THAT BUT THERE MUST BE A MEANS OF JUSTIFICATION, A RESULT AND AN END OF JUSTIFICATION! THE WHOLE GRACE OF GOD IN ITS VARIED FUNCTIONS IS THE FIVE POINTS OF GRACE THAT YOU SEE!

CALVINISM HAS ITS FIVE POINTS OF GRACE AND SO DOES **ARMINIANISM**. THESE TWO GREAT BRANCHES INTO WHICH **PROTESTANT** THEOLOGY HAS BEEN DIVIDED HAVE FALLEN SHORT OF THE APPROPRIATE SYSTEMATIC PATTERN OR ARRANGEMENT OF THEOLOGY THAT REVEALS THE **BEAUTY** OF GOD'S CHARACTER OF **LOVE**. GOD IS LOVE AND LOVE IS **PERFECT**, WHICH TAKES SYSTEMATICISM INTO CONSIDERATION. AND GOD STAKES THE ABSOLUTE PERFECTION OF HIS CHARACTER OR NATURE ON THE **FLAWLESSNESS** AND **PERFECTION** OF THE PLAN HE HAS FORMULATED TO SAVE MAN! THE FIVE POINTS OF GRATUITOUS JUSTIFICATION REVEAL THE PERFECTION OF GOD'S PLAN, THUS ITS EFFICACIOUSNESS IN SAVING MAN, AND THIS EXALTS GOD TO REALLY BE THE **SAVIOUR** OR TO BE **LOVE** ACCORDING TO THE **SPIRITUAL LAW**! IT WOULD BE NOTED THAT THE HALLMARK OF ALL OTHER PLANS IS THEIR FLAWS IN DEALING WITH THE PROBLEM OF MAN, WHILE GOD'S PLAN PREVAILS! AS **ADVENTISM**, THROUGH THE FIVE POINTS GIVEN TO US BY GOD, WE HAVE THE MOST FAMOUS, MOST AUSPICIOUS MOVEMENT ABOUT TO BE BLOSSOMED AND ABOUT TO TAKE OVER THE WHOLE WORLD. LET US THEREFORE HAVE MUCH THANKFULNESS TO GOD AND WORK OVERNIGHT AND SERVE HIM ACCORDING TO THE LIGHT WE HAVE! WITH THE PLAN OF ATONEMENT GIVEN TO US BY GOD, WE END THE WORLD IN OUR TIME!

IN THEIR SEARCH FOR TRUTH, **JONES AND WAGGONER**, THE **1888** MESSENGERS, WERE TO COME UPON THE FIVE POINTS OF SYSTEMATIC JUSTIFICATION IN A SHORT TIME. THE WRITINGS OF WAGGONER REVEAL THAT HE WAS VERSATILE AND NON-CONSERVATVE ENOUGH TO HAVE COME UPON THEM AND HE WOULD HAVE ADVOCATED IT, BUT THE REJECTION OF THE **1888 MESSAGE** BY THE CHURCH AND HIS DISILLUSIONMENT LEADING TO CONJUGAL PROBLEMS PREVENTED HIM! JONES NEEDED THE AID OF WAGGONER ON THIS SO HE WAS NOT ABLE TO GO FAR INTO THE REAL HEART OF THEOLOGY!

NOT ONE OF THE FIVE POINTS OF GOD'S GREAT SACRIFICE (THUSIA) HAS NEGATED A PIN OF ADVENTISM. IN FACT THEY EMBRACE ADVENTIST **ESCHATOLOGY** AND ARRANGE EVERYTHING INTO A BEAUTIFUL CHRONOLOGICAL WHOLE, REVEALING THAT THE VISIONS OF **MRS. WHITE** AND THE ADVOCACIES OF THE EARLY PIONEERS OF OUR FAITH DID IN FACT PURPORT THE OUTER SURFACE OF OUR MOST HOLY FAITH. TODAY, HOWEVER, ACCORDING TO THE BIBLE AND SPIRIT OF PROPHECY, SOME OF GOD'S PEOPLE- THE REAL **REMNANT**, THOSE WHO ARE REBUILDING THE TEMPLE, HAVE PIERCED THE HEART OF **ADVENTISM** AND RICH LIFE GIVING BLOOD HAS BEGUN TO FLOW, REVEALING THAT THE MOST BEAUTIFUL SYSTEM OF GRAND TRUTHS, EFFICACIOUS, SCIENTIFIC OR PRAGMATIC IN ITS NATURE, HAS BEEN GIVEN TO US TO OVERTHROW THE SYSTEMS OF THIS WORLD THAT HAVE SO LONG HELD SWAY! THIS IS THE **1888 MESSAGE**. THE **LATTER RAIN** HAS BEGUN AND THOSE WHO FOLLOW ON TO IT SHALL GO ON TO **SEALED PERFECTION**, LEAVING BEHIND THE CARELESS AND INDIFFERENT. THEY SHALL WALK UP AND DOWN, TO AND FRO ON THE EARTH, TAKING AWAY THE DOMINION OF THE BEAST AND HIS IMAGE AND VINDICATING GOD BEFORE THE WATCHING UNIVERSE!

PROVIDENTIAL GRACE IS THE GRACE OF GOD AS A PROVISION MADE AVAILABLE TO SAVE MAN. THE FOLLOWING IS A CHART OF EXPLANATION. STUDY IT CAREFULLY!

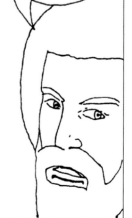

UNDER PROVIDENTIAL GRACE THERE ARE FIVE PARTS OF THE **FORGIVENESS** OF GOD. THESE FIVE ARE THE "**FOR**" OF THE WORD FORGIVENESS:

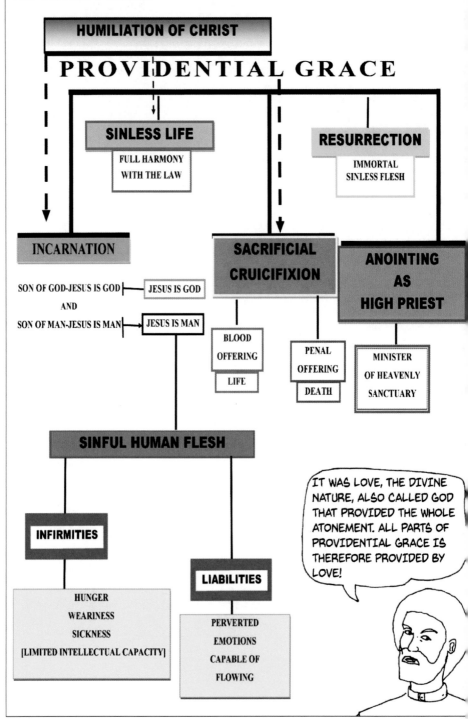

HUMILIATION OF CHRIST

PROVIDENTIAL GRACE

SINLESS LIFE

FULL HARMONY WITH THE LAW

RESURRECTION

IMMORTAL SINLESS FLESH

INCARNATION

SON OF GOD-JESUS IS GOD — JESUS IS GOD

AND

SON OF MAN-JESUS IS MAN — JESUS IS MAN

SACRIFICIAL CRUICIFIXION

BLOOD OFFERING

LIFE

PENAL OFFERING

DEATH

ANOINTING AS HIGH PRIEST

MINISTER OF HEAVENLY SANCTUARY

SINFUL HUMAN FLESH

INFIRMITIES

HUNGER
WEARINESS
SICKNESS
[LIMITED INTELLECTUAL CAPACITY]

LIABILITIES

PERVERTED EMOTIONS CAPABLE OF FLOWING

IT WAS LOVE, THE DIVINE NATURE, ALSO CALLED GOD THAT PROVIDED THE WHOLE ATONEMENT. ALL PARTS OF PROVIDENTIAL GRACE IS THEREFORE PROVIDED BY LOVE!

TEXTUAL RATIFICATION

(A) **INCARNATION**: LUKE 1:26-48; LUKE 2:6-14; MATTHEW 1:18-25; JOHN 1:1,10,14.

GOD- JOHN 1:1; MICAH 5:2; JOHN 20:28; (EXODUS 3:14; JOHN 8:58); (REVELATION 1:11; ISAIAH 48:12; ISAIAH 44:6); HEBREWS 1:8,9; PSALM 45:1-7; ROMANS 9:5; JOHN 5:17,18; (PSALM 68:17-20; EPHESIANS 4:7-10).

MAN- MATTHEW 8:20; MATTHEW 9:6; MATTHEW 24:27; MARK 8:38; LUKE 18:8; JOHN 1:51; JOHN 5:27; ACTS 7:56.

(SINFUL FLESH) -ROMANS 8:3; GALATIANS 4;4,5; HEBREWS 2:14-18.

(B) **SINLESS LIFE**: 1 PETER 2:21,22; 1 JOHN 3:5; ISAIAH 53:9; JOHN 8:46; 2 CORINTHIANS 5:21; HEBREWS 4:15; HEBREWS 7:26; 1 PETER 1:19.
KEEP COMMANDMENTS- JOHN 15:10; JOHN 17:6,12,26; JOHN 14:31; ROMANS 5:19; ISAIAH 42:21.

(C) **SACRIFICIAL CRUCIFIXION**: 1 CORINTHIANS 2:2; GALATIANS 2:20; GALATIANS 3:1.

BLOOD OFFERING (LIFE) -(LEVITICUS 17:11,14); JOHN 6:54,56; ACTS 20:28; ROMANS 3;25; EPHESIANS 1:7; COLOSSIANS 1:20; 1 PETER 1:19; 1 JOHN 1:7; REVELATION 12:11; JOHN 10:10,11,15.
PENAL OFFERING (DEATH)- ISAIAH 53:4,5,8,10,12; PHILIPPIANS 2:8; HEBREWS 2:9; HEBREWS 9:15,22.

(D) **RESURRECTION**: JOHN 11:25; ACTS 17:3,18; PHILIPPIANS 3:10; 2 CORINTHIANS 4;14; ACTS 2;24,;ROMANS 6:9; ROMANS 1:4; ROMANS 10:9; 1 THESSALONIANS 4:14; 1 CORINTHIANS 15:14,17,2.
GLORIFIED FLESH- 1 CORINTHIANS 15:39-44,50-54; JOHN 20:16,17; REVELATION 1:13-15.

(E) **ANNONTING AS HIGH PRIEST**: HEBREWS 2:17; HEBREWS 5:5,6,9,10; HEBREWS 6:19,20; HEBREWS 7:12-28.

HUMILIATION ⟶ HEBREWS 2;6,7,9; PHILIPPIANS 2:6-8; 2 CORINTHIANS 8:9; LUKE 2:7; MATTHEW 27:28; ACTS 8:33.

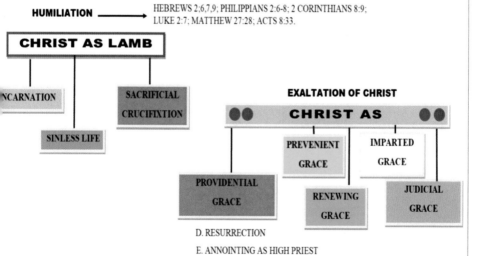

CHRIST AS LAMB

NCARNATION

SACRIFICIAL CRUCIFIXTION

SINLESS LIFE

EXALTATION OF CHRIST

CHRIST AS

PREVENIENT GRACE

IMPARTED GRACE

PROVIDENTIAL GRACE

RENEWING GRACE

JUDICIAL GRACE

D. RESURRECTION

E. ANNOINTING AS HIGH PRIEST

BOTH THE HUMILIATION AND EXALTATION OF CHRIST FOR THE SAKE OF THE SAINTS ARE MADE AVAILABLE IN *THE ATONEMENT*. WE TOO ARE HUMILIATED IN CHRIST, THAT IN HIM WE MAY BE EXALTED!

FIN

PREPARED AND PUBLISHED BY THE SERVICES OF THUSIA (SDA). JANUARY, 1986.

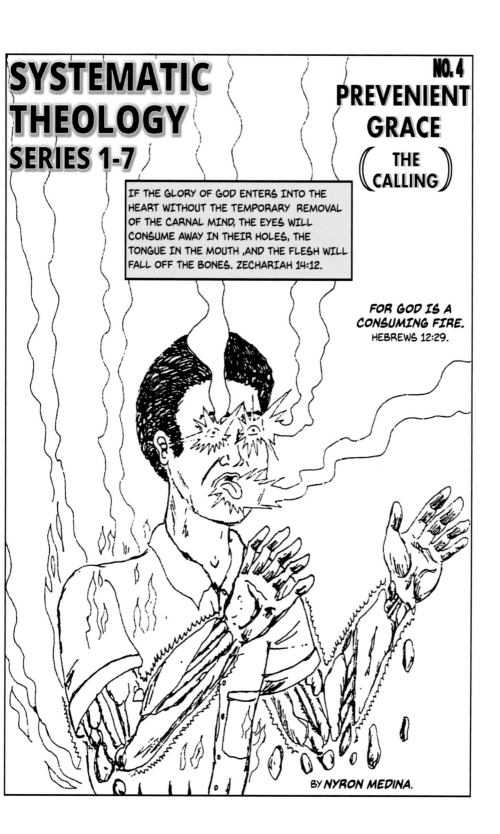

PILLAR FOUR: PREVENIENT GRACE (THE CALLING)

THE VALUE OF THE SECOND POINT IN THE FIVE POINTS OF GRACE CAN NEVER BE UNDER ESTIMATED WITHOUT PUNITY. THIS GREAT TRUTH OF **PREVENIENT GRACE** DISCOVERED IN ITS PRIMITIVE FORM BY **JOHN WESLEY** HAS NOW BEEN GIVEN TO US BY GOD IN ITS DEVELOPED FORM SHOWING ITS SIX PARTS, TWO OF WHICH ARE MAN'S RESPONSE! THE NECESSITY OF PREVENIENT GRACE IS THAT IT IS THE ONLY TRUE CONDITION OF JUSTIFICATION; IF RENEWAL IS TO OCCUR IN THE MAN, IT MUST FIRST BE PRECEDED BY A **CALLING** FROM GOD IN WHICH THE MAN RESPONDS. THUS, PREVENIENT GRACE IS **SYNERGISTIC**! PREVENIENT GRACE IS THE **GRACE OF GOD** PLACED INTO OUR HEARTS FOR CONVICTION BEFORE WE ARE CONVERTED, AND THIS EXERCISE OF GOD'S OWN INITIATIVE MUST BE REACTED TO BY THE APPROPRIATE **HUMAN RESPONSE** OF **REPENTANCE** AND **BELIEVING** IF WE ARE TO BE JUSTIFIED! IN THIS EXERCISE GOD MUST FIRST TEMPORARILY REMOVE THE CARNAL MIND OF MAN AT WHICH FOR A BRIEF WHILE THE MAN HAS **NIHILATION** (WHICH MEANS NO HOLY OR CARNAL VALUES). THEN GOD, BY THE PLACING OF FAITH MUST TEMPORARILY PLACE THE DIVINE MIND!

BY THE TEMPORARY PLACING OF THE DIVINE MIND IN THE MAN, THIS BRINGS CONVICTION OF SIN AND OF RIGHTEOUSNESS! AT THAT MOMENT, THE MAN NOW SEES GOD TO BE LOVE, AND SIN TO BE EVIL, AND AS HE LOOKS A LITTLE LONGER TO SEE THE PLEASURES OF **LOVE**, HE SLOWLY BEGINS TO DEVELOP AN APPETITE FOR IT! AT THIS TIME, IF HE **REPENTS**, WHICH IS REJECTING THE CARNAL MIND AS NOT LOVE, AND HE REJECTS ITS RULERSHIP IN HIS SOUL, AND **BELIEVES** OR ACCEPTS AS TRUTH TO REIGN IN HIS SOUL AND EXISTENCE THE DIVINE MIND, GOD CRUCIFIES THE CARNAL MIND WHICH IS **NON-IMPUTING** IT TO THE MAN, AND **IMPUTES** THE DIVINE MIND OF RIGHTEOUSNESS TO THE MAN, AND AT THAT MOMENT HE IS JUSTIFIED!

NOT ALL MEN WILL REPENT AND BELIEVE. ALTHOUGH THERE IS NO **REASON** FOR THIS, THE **CAUSE** OF THEIR TURNING AWAY IS THE RECONSIDERING OF SELF AS LOVE AGAIN, IN PLACE OF THE **LOVE** OF THE DIVINE MIND OF GOD!

IT IS OF MUCH NECESSITY THAT GOD TEMPORARILY REMOVE THE CARNAL MIND AND THAT **NIHILATION** COMES BEFORE THE TEMPORARY PLACING OF THE DIVINE MIND, FOR IF THE DIVINITY OF GOD WERE TO MEET THE CARNAL MIND IN THE MAN'S MIND, THE **GLORY** OF THIS **RIGHTEOUSNESS** THAT CONSUMES SIN WILL CONSUME THAT MAN THAT HAS THAT SIN IN HIM (SEE ZECHARIAH 14:12, HEBREWS 12:29 AND 2 SAMUEL 6:6,7). THE TEMPORARY EXISTENCE OF THE DIVINE MIND IN THE MIND DOES NOT MAKE THE MAN RIGHTEOUS AT THAT TIME, BECAUSE IT IS ONLY WHEN HE REPENTS AND BELIEVES AND GOD IMPUTES THIS MIND TO THE MAN, THAT HE IS **SUBJECTIVELY MADE RIGHTEOUS**, BECAUSE **JUSTIFICATION** IS BY **IMPUTATION** AND NOT BY **INFUSATION**! THE TEMPORARY ABSENCE OF THE CARNAL MIND FROM IN THE MAN DOES NOT PURGE HIM FROM THAT DEFILEMENT, FOR IT IS ONLY WHEN THE MAN REPENTS AND BELIEVES THAT GOD DOES NOT IMPUTE THIS SIN UNTO THE MAN, PURGING HIM! THESE THINGS WILL BE DEALT WITH IN THE NEXT STUDY (#5).

GOD HAS GIVEN TO US THE TRUTH ABOUT PREVENIENT GRACE TO ENSURE THAT OUR PREACHING IS NOT OF A HIT AND MISS MANNER, BUT THAT WE MAY KNOW WHEN WE SHOULD PREACH, OR THE NECESSITY, BEFORE PREACHING, THAT WE MAY NOT WASTE OUR TIME WITH MUCH WORDS! BY THE RIGHT ACTION OR WORDS, WE COULD (FROM GOD'S INITIATIVE) CAUSE THE CARNAL MIND TO BE TEMPORARILY REMOVED THAT OUR MESSAGE WOULD BE SURE TO BE HEARD WHETHER THE PEOPLE WILL ACCEPT OR REJECT IT! WE, BY THIS, EITHER CONVERT PEOPLE, OR HEAP COALS OF FIRE UPON THEIR HEADS UNTO THE DAY OF JUDGEMENT! BUT THE PRIMARY POINT OF PREVENIENT GRACE IS THAT WE MAY NOT CAST OUR PEARLS BEFORE SWINES!

NO MAN CAN COME UNTO GOD BY HIMSELF. MAN HAS NO APPETITE FOR GOD. IT IS GOD THAT MUST FIRST CALL MAN, AND MAN MUST RESPOND!

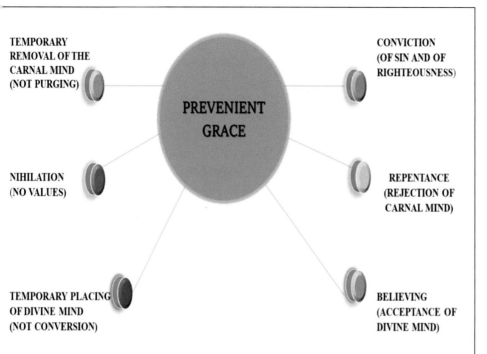

TEMPORARY
REMOVAL OF THE
CARNAL MIND
(NOT PURGING)

CONVICTION
(OF SIN AND OF
RIGHTEOUSNESS)

PREVENIENT
GRACE

NIHILATION
(NO VALUES)

REPENTANCE
(REJECTION OF
CARNAL MIND)

TEMPORARY PLACING
OF DIVINE MIND
(NOT CONVERSION)

BELIEVING
(ACCEPTANCE OF
DIVINE MIND)

a. TEMPORARY REMOVAL OF CARNAL MIND:
ACTS 13:7; ACTS 13:16; ROMANS 8:6-8; ROMANS 3:11; JOB 35:9-11.

b. NIHILATION:
ACTS 8:26-34; ACTS 14:8-14; ACTS 21:33-40; HOSEA 5:1.

c. TEMPORARY PLACING OF DIVINE MIND:
PSALM 51:1-19; DANIEL 3:28; HOSEA 11:4.

d. CONVICTION:
TITUS 1:9; JOHN 16:8; ACTS 2:37; ACTS 16:29,30; PSALM 51:4; ACTS 8:37.

e. REPENTANCE:
LUKE 24:47; ACTS 5:31; 2 TIMOTHY 2:25; 2 PETER 3:9; MARK 1:15; ACTS 17:30; REVELATION 3:19.

f. BELIEVING:
GENESIS 15:6; ROMANS 4:3; JAMES 2:23; ROMANS 10:10; JOHN 20:31; JOHN 3:36; JOHN 3:15,16; ACTS 13:39; ACTS 16:31.

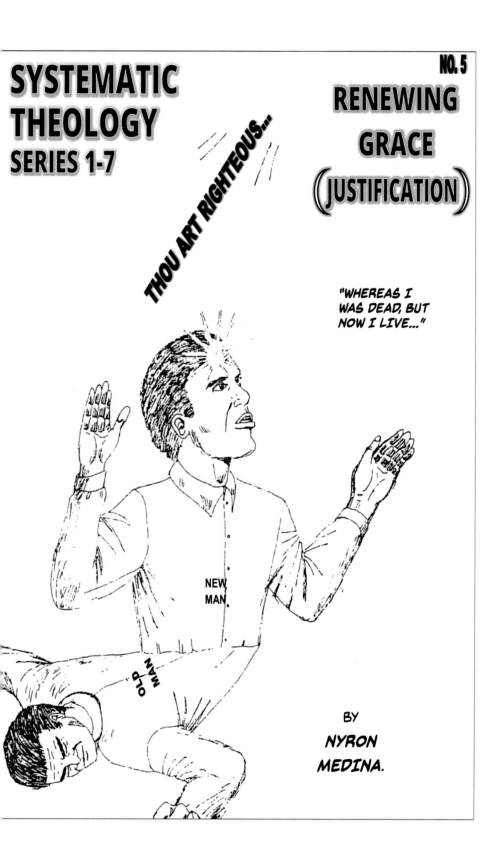

A COURSE IN
SYSTEMATIC THEOLOGY

BY *NYRON MEDINA*

PILLAR FIVE : JUSTIFICATION

THE FIFTH OF THE **SEVEN PILLARS OF SYSTEMATIC THEOLOGY** IS **RENEWING GRACE**, OR AS COMMONLY CALLED **JUSTIFICATION.** THIS IS THE THIRD POINT OF THE **FIVE POINTS OF GRACE** WHICH IS THE WHOLE, GREAT, GRAND ATONEMENT! JUSTIFICATION IS THE TRANSFORMATIVE CENTER OF THE ATONEMENT BECAUSE IT IS THE **CHANGE** ON WHICH HANGS THE LAST TWO POINTS OF GRACE, AND IT IS THE OBJECT OF THE FIRST TWO POINTS! (THE SACRIFICIAL CRUCIFIXION IS THE PROVIDENTIAL CENTER OF THE ATONEMENT, BECAUSE WITHOUT IT THE SIN PROBLEM WOULD NOT HAVE BEEN ABLE TO BE DEALT WITH). IF **SANCTIFICATION** IS TO BE REALIZED OR THE **BLOTTING OUT** OF PAST SINS ACCOMPLISHED, IT MUST BE PRECEDED BY AN INNER RENEWAL CALLED JUSTIFICATION!

JUSTIFICATION HAS BEEN THE MOST ABUSED DOCTRINE IN THE HISTORY OF CHRISTIANITY. THE **REFORMATION** STARTED OVER WHAT CONSTITUTED IT, AND WILL END BY PROVING ITS ABILITY TO DELIVER MAN FROM THE **SUNDAY LAW** TRANSGRESSION!

WHAT IS JUSTIFICATION? IT IS THE WORK OF CHRIST IN US, IT IS GOD MAKING THE MAN WHO BELIEVES RIGHTEOUS IN FACT AND IN ACTUAL TRUTH! THE WORD JUSTIFICATION IS THE LATIN WHICH MEANS "RIGHTEOUS TO MAKE" OR "TO MAKE RIGHTEOUS". IN THE BIBLE THIS IS ONLY USED IN A **SUBJECTIVE** SENSE! GOD IS DECLARED TO BE RIGHTEOUS BECAUSE HE IS RIGHTEOUS IN FACT, AND NO MAN THAT HAS SIN IN HIM WHICH HE HOLDS AS VALUABLE IS EVER ESTEEMED RIGHTEOUS!

BUT THIS IS THE WAY IN WHICH GOD JUSTIFIES MAN! UNDER **PREVENIENT GRACE** GOD TEMPORARILY REMOVES THE CARNAL MIND (THIS IS NOT SLAYING IT) AND AS THE MAN IS IN THE STATE OF **NIHILATION** GOD PLACES IN HIS HEART THE DIVINE MIND OF RIGHTEOUSNESS TO CONVICT HIM OF SIN AND OF RIGHTEOUSNESS (THIS IS NOT CONVERSION AS YET). AS THE MAN SEES THE BEAUTY AND PLEASURE OF LOVE, AND WANTS IT TO BECOME THE BASIS OF HIS NEW EXISTENCE AND EXPERIENCE, AND AS HE THUS **REPENTS**, WHICH IS REJECTING THE CARNAL MIND, AND AT THE SAME TIME HE **BELIEVES** OR ACCEPTS THE DIVINE MIND OF RIGHTEOUSNESS AS **LOVE**-THE TRUE **IDEAL** WHICH HE WANTS TO NOW RULE HIS EXISTENCE-GOD CEASES TO COUNT THE CARNAL MIND AS THE MAN'S OWN, AND COUNTS (OR IMPUTES) THE DIVINE MIND OR RIGHTEOUSNESS AS THE MAN'S OWN. THIS IS JUSTIFYING THE MAN!

THE **NON-IMPUTATION OF SIN** WHICH IS THE DEATH OF THE CARNAL MIND (OR UNRIGHTEOUSNESS IN THE SOUL), AND THE **IMPUTATION OF THE DIVINE MIND** WHICH IS RIGHTEOUSNESS IN THE SOUL AS BELONGING TO THE SOUL IS JUSTIFICATION! THE RIGHTEOUSNESS WAS PLACED IN THE SOUL FOR CONVICTION, AND WHEN THE VALUES OF THE CARNAL MIND WERE REJECTED AND THE RIGHTEOUSNESS WAS ACCEPTED, GOD, IN HIS OWN MIND **ESTEEMED** THIS RIGHTEOUSNESS AS BELONGING TO THE SOUL, AND THIS IS WHAT MAKES THE SOUL RIGHTEOUS! SO THEN, JUSTIFICATION IS BY **GOD'S** ESTIMATION, IT IS BY GOD **ESTEEMING** IN HIS MIND THAT THE MAN IS RIGHTEOUS AND THIS MAKES HIM SO IN FACT, THAT HE IS NOW A **BORN AGAIN, REGENERATED, CONVERTED** HUMAN BEING! JUSTIFICATION IS AN **ESTIMATION** THAT **MAKES**! THE RIGHTEOUSNESS IN THE SOUL FOR CONVICTION IS MERELY MADE THE PERSONAL POSSESSION OF THE SOUL, THUS HE IS **SUBJECTIVELY** RIGHTEOUS!

THUS, WHEN CHRIST WHO IS OUR RIGHTEOUSNESS IS MADE THE **PERSONAL SAVIOUR** OF THE SOUL WE ARE JUSTIFIED! THE RIGHTEOUSNESS STILL RESIDING WITH THE **TRUTH** OR **FAITH** THAT CHRIST IS, WHEN ATTRIBUTED AS OURS, THIS IS HOW FAITH IS ACCOUNTED TO US FOR RIGHTEOUSNESS! JUSTIFICATION IS A MAKING RIGHTEOUS IN REALITY BY GOD'S GRACIOUS ESTIMATION!

OUR RIGHTEOUSNESS IS HERE ON EARTH IN CHRIST WHO IS IN US **WHO** ARE TURNED UNTO GOD!

THE DIVINE NATURE WHICH IS THE RIGHTEOUSNESS OF GOD, THE SPIRITUAL LAW, THE LOVE OF GOD HIMSELF, IS IMPUTED INTO US, BECOMING THE ACTUAL SUBJECTIVE POSSESSION OF THE PERSON WHEN HE BELIEVES. THIS IS JUSTIFICATION! THE TRANSFORMATION OF THE PERSON FROM THE SIN OF THE CARNAL MIND TO THE RIGHTEOUSNESS OF GOD IS JUSTIFICATION! GOD HIMSELF GIVES HIMSELF AS AN INDWELLING GIFT TO THE REPENTANT PERSON. THIS IS THE GIFT OF THE SPIRIT IN OUR HEARTS, IT IS OUR SUBJECTIVE JUSTIFICATION!

CONVERSION IS JUSTIFICATION. THE PURGING OR CLEANSING OF THE SOUL TEMPLE FROM INNER DEFILEMENT IS JUSTIFICATION. THUS JUSTIFICATION IS WHAT CHRIST DOES **IN** THE SOUL, IT IS AN EFFECTUAL CHANGE!

THE POINT ABOUT JUSTIFICATION IS THAT GOD WILL NEVER ACCEPT ONE WHO YET HOLDS CARNAL VALUES AS RIGHTEOUS, THUS ANY CHANGE (NO MATTER HOW IT IS IDENTIFIED IN THE SCRIPTURES), ONCE IT IS THE DIVINE WORK OF CHANGING THE SPIRITUAL STATE, IS TRULY JUSTIFICATION!

THE NATURE OF JUSTIFICATION

A. IT IS THE NON-IMPUTATION OF SIN (THE CARNAL MIND). PSALM 32:2; ROMANS 4:8; 2 CORINTHIANS 5:19; LUKE 3:3; LUKE 24:47; ACTS 2:38; ROMANS 6:2-7.

B. IT IS THE IMPUTATION OF FAITH FOR RIGHTEOUSNESS. GENESIS 15:6; ROMANS 4:3,5,6,9,11,12,22; GALATIANS 3:6; GALATIANS 2:16.

C. IT IS THE TRANSFORMATION OR RENEWING OF THE MIND BY IMPUTATION, IT IS THE GIFT OF THE DIVINE MIND. PSALM 51:10; TITUS 3:5; ROMANS 12:2; PHILIPPIANS 2:5; COLOSSIANS 3:9,10; EPHESIANS 4:22-24; (PSALM 119:151; PSALM 51:6.) ROMANS 8:4,6.

D. IT IS A SUBJECTIVE SUBSTITUTION OR IT IS VICARIOUSLY SUBJECTIVE. (ROMANS 3:28,31; ISAIAH 51:7; ROMANS 8:4). 2 CORINTHIANS 5:17; 2 CORINTHIANS 4:6,7. (EPHESIANS 2:1,5,10; ROMANS 4:17). GALATIANS 2:19,20; GALATIANS 3:2,3,6,11; 1 JOHN 1:9.

E. CHRIST'S DIVINE NATURE, HIS RIGHTEOUSNESS IS COUNTED INTO US AS OUR SUBJECTIVE JUSTIFICATION. (ROMANS 3:22; 1 CORINTHIANS 1:30; 2 PETER 1:4; EPHESIANS 3:17).

F. IT IS THE VERY GOD OF LOVE, JESUS HIMSELF THAT IS IMPUTED INTO THE BELIEVER. (1 JOHN 4:15,16; 1 JOHN 5:20; GALATIANS 2:16,20; ROMANS 5:1,5).

G. IT IS BY GOD'S GRACE. JOHN 1:16; ROMANS 5:15,17,21; ROMANS 11:5,6; GALATIANS 2:21; EPHESIANS 3:7; EPHESIANS 2:5,8.

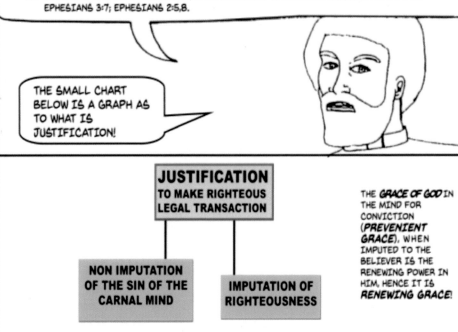

THE SMALL CHART BELOW IS A GRAPH AS TO WHAT IS JUSTIFICATION!

JUSTIFICATION
TO MAKE RIGHTEOUS
LEGAL TRANSACTION

THE *GRACE OF GOD* IN THE MIND FOR CONVICTION (*PREVENIENT GRACE*), WHEN IMPUTED TO THE BELIEVER IS THE RENEWING POWER IN HIM, HENCE IT IS *RENEWING GRACE*!

NON IMPUTATION OF THE SIN OF THE CARNAL MIND

IMPUTATION OF RIGHTEOUSNESS

HERE ARE SOME POINTS TO NOTE:

A. JUSTIFICATION BY FAITH MEANS THAT FAITH, WHICH CONTAINS RIGHTEOUSNESS, COMMUNICATES IT TO THE HEART FOR UNDERSTANDING, CONVICTION AND IMPUTATION IF THE SOUL BELIEVES!

B. IT IS SOLELY GOD BY HIS GRACE OR PROPITIATIOUS NATURE THAT JUSTIFIES US WHEN THE APPROPRIATE CONDITIONS ARE FULFILLED.

C. JUSTIFICATION BY IMPUTATION SIMPLY MEANS THAT IT IS ONLY WHEN GOD COUNTS THE RIGHTEOUSNESS AS OURS THAT WE ARE JUSTIFIED, NO OTHER TIME.

D. JUSTIFICATION IS THE BEGINNING OF ETERNAL LIFE IN THE SOUL BY IMPUTATION.

E. JUSTIFICATION IS A LEGAL (RIGHT) TRANSACTION, THE MINISTRATION OF DIVINE JUSTICE AND THIS MAKES US LEGALISTS (RIGHTISTS).

PREPARED AND PUBLISHED BY THE SERVICES OF THUSIA (SDA). JANUARY, 1986.

PILLAR SIX: SANCTIFICATION

BY FAR THE MOST WONDERFUL TOPIC IN SYSTEMATIC THEOLOGY AND THE ONE EVERY CHRISTIAN SHOULD BE CONTINUALLY DWELLING IN IS **IMPARTED GRACE** OR THE DOCTRINE OF **SANCTIFICATION**. IT IS THE PRECIOUS TRUTHS OF SANCTIFICATION THAT REFRESH US, GIVING US **HOPE** OF OVERCOMING ALL SINS, AND, OUR MINDS ARE FILLED WITH THE HOLY PLEASURE OF THE BEAUTY OF HOLINESS! **MR. WESLEY**, MORE THAN ANY PROTESTANT REFORMER, DEVELOPED THIS DOCTRINE FROM THE SACRED SCRIPTURES INTO ITS TRUE LEGAL SETTING! NOTWITHSTANDING THAT HIS TEACHINGS WERE ATTENDED WITH SOME ERRORS, HIS GENERAL IDEA OF **PERFECTION**, AND OF DELIVERANCE FROM PRACTICED SINS WAS NEAR THE WHOLESOME TRUTH; AND NOW, IN THE TIME OF THE END, THE TRUE DOCTRINE OF SANCTI-FICATION WHICH OPERATES WITHIN THE CONTEXT OF SINFREENESS,...

THAT HAS BEEN ENDOWED UPON THE BELIEVER BY **JUSTIFICATION**, HAS BEEN DELIVERED BY ANGELS TO **THUSIA**. SO LET US REAP THE MAXIMUM BENEFITS EXPECTED OF US IN SUCH LIGHT, AND BRING CHRIST BACK TO THE EARTH! SANCTIFICATION IS THAT PART OF THE WHOLE **ATONEMENT** CALLED IMPARTED GRACE, BECAUSE THE GRACES OF THE ATONEMENT ARE PROGRESSIVELY IMPARTED TO THE HEART TO SATISFY THE CONSCIENCE WITH VIEWS OF THE LOVE OF GOD, MAKING THE MAN LOSE VALUE FOR THE VARIATIONS OF THE CARNAL MIND, WHILE NOT HOLDING ON TO THEM AS LOVING VALUES AND NOT PRACTICING THEM!

RIGHTEOUSNESS BY FAITH INCLUDES SANCTIFICATION

RIGHTEOUSNESS OR JUSTIFICATION BY FAITH INCLUDES SANCTIFICATION AS A TAGALONG! IT IS FAITH THAT COMMUNICATES RIGHTEOUSNESS TO THE HEART FOR CONVICTION, SO THAT WHEN THE SOUL REPENTS AND BELIEVES, GOD IMPUTES THE RIGHTEOUSNESS TO THE SOUL MAKING HIM RIGHTEOUS, OR MAKING THE RIGHTEOUSNESS BELONG TO THE SOUL. THUS THE MAN IS JUSTIFIED! GOD ESTEEMS THE MAN RIGHTEOUS BY ATTRIBUTING HIS RIGHTEOUSNESS OF FAITH TO THE SOUL! TO CONTINUE THIS PROCESS WHICH IS CALLED SANCTIFICATION, GOD MUST NOT NOW JUSTIFY THE SOUL FOR THE FIRST TIME AS IF THAT WAS NOT DONE BEFORE. GOD MUST NOW **CONTINUE** THIS SERVICE IN THE SOUL BY CONTINUALLY IMPARTING FAITH FOR RIGHTEOUSNESS INTO THE SOUL. SO THAT AS HE CONTINUALLY REPENTS AND BELIEVES, GOD'S CONTINUOUS UNBROKEN ESTIMATION OF THE MAN AS RIGHTEOUS IS HIS SANCTIFICATION!

THUS THE SAME PROCESS THAT HAPPENS IN JUSTIFICATION, WITH THE EXCEPTION OF TRANSFORMING THE MAN OUT OF SUBJECTIVE SINS INTO RIGHTEOUSNESS SUBJECTIVELY, HAPPENS IN SANCTIFICATION, AND, AS JUSTIFICATION IS BY FAITH IN THE SENSE OF **COMMUNICATION**, SO IS SANCTIFICATION! AS FAITH PLACES RIGHTEOUSNESS INTO THE SOUL FOR IMPUTATION, SO IT PLACES RIGHTEOUSNESS INTO THE SOUL FOR CONTINUAL UNBROKEN IMPUTATION (BUT NOT TO DELIVER FROM PRACTICED SINS, BECAUSE THEY ARE NOT BEING PRACTICED BY THE CONVERTED MAN) AND THIS IS OUR SANCTIFICATION! THUS RIGHTEOUSNESS BY FAITH IS BOTH JUSTIFICATION AND SANCTIFICATION!

SANCTIFICATION DOES NOT CONVERT THE MAN OR REGENERATE HIM. IT DOES NOT DO THE WORK OF JUSTIFICATION. IT IS MERELY JUSTIFICATION CONTINUED BUT IN A SUBJECTIVE SINFREE CONTEXT! SANCTIFICATION IS THE MAINTENENCE OF RIGHTEOUSNESS, OBEDIENCE TO THE LAW OF GOD IN THE SOUL, BY UNBROKEN IMPUTATION OF GOD! UNDER JUSTIFICATION THE CARNAL MIND IS NO LONGER IMPUTED AS BELONGING TO THE REPENTANT. THE RIGHTEOUSNESS IN HIM WHICH IS COUNTED AS HIS OWN DETERMINES HIM A NEW *SINFREE* CREATURE! JUSTIFICATION, THEN, CONFERRED SINFREENESS TO THE BELIEVER. HE NO LONGER HOLDS THE GODS OF THE CARNAL MIND AS VALUES OR AS LOVE IN HIS PRESENT CONSCIOUSNESS. THUS HE HAS NO SIN, BUT IN HIS MEMORY ARE ACCOUNTS OF ALL THOSE FALSE GODS FOR WHICH HE HAS NOT YET SEEN THE TRUTH, AS OPPOSED TO THEIR FALSE CLAIMS. AS GOD IMPARTS DIALECTUAL FAITH TO HIM WHICH OBVIOUSLY SMASHES, EXPOSES OR BRINGS TO CLEAR VIEW THE VANITY, EMPTINESS AND DISSATISFACTION OF THE FALSE GODS OF THE CARNAL MIND, SHOWING THE MAN THAT THERE IS NO PLEASURE OR SATISFACTION IN THEM AND THAT THEY ROB HIM OF MEANINGFULNESS OF HIS EXISTENCE, THE MAN REJECTS THEM (REPENTANCE) AND BELIEVES THE FAITH FOR ITS RIGHTEOUSNESS. HE BELIEVES THE FACT THAT GOD IS LOVE ABOVE ALL THE FALSE GODS AND THAT GOD ALONE COULD SATISFY HIM. THEN GOD IMPUTES THE RIGHTEOUSNESS TO THE MAN, MAINTAINING RIGHTEOUSNESS IN HIS SOUL! THIS IS SANCTIFICATION! OBSERVE THAT IT DID NOT INVOLVE THE MAN FALLING INTO SIN AT ALL, FOR IT IS IN THE REALM OF SINFREENESS! IF THE MAN FALLS INTO SIN AGAIN THEN HE HAS TO BE JUSTIFIED AGAIN. THUS SANCTIFICATION IS THE MAINTENANCE OF RIGHTEOUSNESS IN THE SOUL!

UNBROKENNESS

UNDER SANCTIFICATION THERE IS TO BE CONTINUOUS AND UNBROKEN CONVICTION, REPENTANCE, BELIEVING AND GOD'S ACT OF IMPUTATION! BY CONTINUALLY IMPARTING GRACE TO THE SOUL, THE MAN IS CONTINUALLY CONVICTED, HE CONTINUALLY REJECTS THE CARNAL MIND'S VALUES (OR REPENTS) AND CONTINUALLY BELIEVES OR ACCEPTS AS TRUTH THE *LOVE* OF GOD PRESENTED IN OPPOSITION TO THE CARNAL MIND. THUS GOD CONTINUALLY IMPUTES THIS FAITH FOR ITS RIGHTEOUSNESS UNTO THE SOUL!

DEVELOP FAITH, WORKS, CULTURING AFFECTIONS

UNDER SANCTIFICATION IS PERPETUATED THE MATURING OF ONE'S FAITH AND THE DEVELOPMENT OF GOOD WORKS TO SUIT THE MATURING FAITH. TEMPTATIONS, WHICH ARE NOT SIN, ARE FACED WITH FAITH, AND THE PATH OF DUTY (WHICH IS FAITH) TO WALK IN, IS FOLLOWED, THAT ITS LOVE MIGHT BE REVEALED IN AND FROM THE SOUL, THUS THE MAN FULFILS THE LAW! WHEREAS THE SOUL DID WORKS THAT DID NOT REVEAL THE LOVE OF GOD BEFORE (SOME BEING PLAINLY EVIL AND SOME, WHILE GOOD IN THEIR SHAPE, FORM OR OPERATION, WERE VOID OF FAITH THUS THEY WERE EVIL), NOW UNDER SANCTIFICATION, WORKS IN WHICH THE LOVE OF GOD IS REVEALED MUST BE PROSECUTED, AND NOT ONLY THIS, IT IS THE INTENTION OF THE FAITH WITH ITS LOVE TO CAUSE DIFFERENT AND NEW KINDS OF EMOTIONAL AFFECTIONS TO FLOW IN THE FLESH (THIS IS CALLED THE SANCTIFICATION OF THE BODY)! UNDER SANCTIFICATION NO *BODY OF SINS* OR PERVERTED EMOTIONS ARE TO FLOW IN THE BODY, FOR THE FAITH AND LOVE DRAWS AND CULTURES THE AFFECTIONS TO HEAVENLY AND SPIRITUAL THINGS, SO THAT THE SOUL COMES TO EMOTIONALLY LOVE (AGAPE) HOLY THINGS NATURALLY! THUS THE AFFECTIONS ARE NOT ONLY FOR HEAVENLY THINGS, BUT IT ALSO DEVELOPS A DISTASTE FOR WORLDLY THINGS. THE SOUL MUST REACH THIS STAGE AT LEAST, BEFORE ITS PEACE CONTINUES, AND IT IS SURE THAT IT HATES UNHOLY OR SINFUL THINGS WHEN THE SOUL RECOILS FROM EVIL. THUS WHEN SATAN COMES, HE FINDS NOTHING IN THE SOUL THAT APPEALS TO HIS TEMPTATIONS!

SANCTIFICATION WITHIN THE STATE OF SINFREE PERFECTION

IT IS WRONG TO ASSUME THAT THE RISING OUT OF SIN AND A FALLING BACK INTO IT AGAIN AND A RISING OUT AGAIN ON A CONTINUOUS SCALE, WHICH SUPPOSEDLY BECOMES LESS IN FREQUENCY AS TIME PASSES, CONSTITUTE SANCTIFICATION, FOR THOUGH THIS MAY HAPPEN AGAIN AND AGAIN IN THE SOUL IT REVEALS THAT THE MAN IS REALLY BEING JUSTIFIED AND FALLING INTO SIN AGAIN, WHICH IS NOT BEING SANCTIFIED! SANCTIFICATION, WHICH IS THE MAINTENANCE OF RIGHTEOUSNESS IN THE SOUL, DOES NOT IN THE LEAST WAY INCLUDE A FALLING INTO SIN BUT A DELIVERANCE FROM IT IN THE REALM OF SINFREENESS! SANCTIFICATION DOES NOT CONFER PERFECTION AS A FIRST INSTANCE TO THE SOUL, THIS IS WHAT IS ACCOMPLISHED BY JUSTIFICATION AND IS CONTINUED BY SANCTIFICATION!

SO THEN, THE MAN IS MADE SINFREE PERFECT BY JUSTIFICATION, AND SANCTIFICATION MAINTAINS THIS IN HIM, BY REMOVING THE ASSUMED CREDIBILITY OF THE FALSE VALUES, SUBSTITUTING TRANSCENDENT LOVE IN THEIR PLACES AND THUS DIRECTING THE SOUL INTO THE RIGHT THOUGHTS, WORDS AND ACTIONS, SO HE WOULD NOT FALL INTO SIN BY BEING TEMPTED!

SANCTIFICATION MADE A REALITY BY HOPE

THE DOCTRINE OF SANCTIFICATION IS INSEPARABLY BOUND TO THE DOCTRINE OF **HOPE**! FOR FAITH GIVES HOPE AND HOPE KEEPS US IN FAITH AND LOVE, HOPE BEING A CREATED HUMAN RESPONSE! TO HOPE FOR SALVATION IS TO HAVE A MENTAL APPETITE TO SEE THE LOVE OF GOD DELIVERING THE SOUL FROM SIN! HOPE, THEN, IS THE APPETITE TO SEE THE LOVE OF GOD THAT IS PLACED IN THE SOUL BY FAITH! WHEN FAITH PLACES THIS APPETITE THERE, WHICH IS THE HUNGERING AND THIRSTING FOR RIGHTEOUSNESS OR THE WILLINGNESS TO DO THE WILL OF GOD, GOD, WHO PROMISES TO SATISY THIS, THROUGH HIS SPIRIT SENDS MORE FAITH IN WHICH IS LOVE, AND THIS NOT ONLY SATISFIES THE APPETITE OF HOPE, BUT STRENGTHENS IT AGAIN, MAKING IT BECOME MORE CHRONIC THAT GOD HAS TO REVEAL MORE AGAIN IN A NEVER ENDING PROCESS! THIS HOPE, MAINTAINED AND STRENGTHENED IN THE SOUL IS WHAT GIVES THE SPIRIT LEEWAY TO THE CONTINUOUS REVEALING OF LOVE IN THE SOUL (FOR GOD WILL FORCE HIMSELF UPON NO MAN), AND THIS IS THE CONTINUOUS MAINTAINING OF LOVE IN THE SOUL OR SANCTIFICATION!

SO THEN, SANCTIFICATION IN ITS CREATED HUMAN REPSONSE LEVEL IS THE MAINTENANCE OF LOVE OR RIGHTEOUSNESS IN THE SOUL BY THE SPIRIT'S ANSWERING OR FULFILLING HOPE, WHICH HE FIRST PUT THERE! SO THEN HOPE CAUSES OUR SANCTIFICATION, AND HOPE SAVES US! OUR SANCTIFICATION IS MADE A TRANSPIRING REALITY BY THE PRESENCE OF HOPE IN US THAT HAS BEEN CREATED BY THE SPIRIT OF FAITH!

WE ARE TO PRAY WITHOUT CEASING! THIS PRAYER IS NOT THAT WHICH IS THE OCCASIONAL ADDRESS TO GOD. THIS PRAYER IS THE PRAYER OF TRUE MEDITATION! EVERY MOMENT OUR MINDS ARE THINKING IN A NONSTOPABLE WAY, IF WE CONTINUALLY HAVE AN APPETITE TO SEE THE LOVE OF GOD, WITH GOD IN OUR PRESENT CONSCIOUSNESS AS THE PRETHESIS OR A PRIORI, THEN WE ARE MEDITATING AS PRAYER, AND EVERY THOUGHT THAT COMES INTO OUR MINDS WILL BE FROM THE *SPIRITUAL LAW* CONTINUALLY, ALWAYS KEEPING GOD (THE LIVING SPIRITUAL LAW) EVER BEFORE OUR MINDS! THIS IS REMAINING IN GOD THROUGH UNCEASING PRAYER WHICH IS MEDITATION AS A FORMAL ADDRESS TO GOD! THUS SANCTIFICATION, BY BEING PERPETUATED BECAUSE OF HOPE IN THE HEART, IS MADE AN ACTUALITY THROUGH SECRET UNCEASING PRAYER WHICH IS TRUE MEDITATION! HOPE WILL BE CONSTANT IN THE MAN AND THUS PRAYER SHALL ALWAYS TRANSCEND FROM HIS HEART. THE APPETITE OF HOPE DEVELOPS BECOMING MAGNANIMOUSLY CHRONIC BECAUSE OF MEDITATION WITH GOD AS THE PRETHESIS IN THE MIND OR FORMALLY ADDRESSING GOD! SUCH AN APPETITE COULD ENDURE HUNGER, WEARINESS, DELAY AND ALL SORTS OF PERSECUTION...

AND AS IT REMAINS, GOD CONTINUALLY FEEDS IT WITH LOVE, SATISFYING IT, YET STILL STRENGTHENING IT UNTIL ALL THE MAN RECEIVES IS FAITH AND LOVE FROM GOD! THIS MAN HAS REACHED SEALED PERFECTION! SINCE THE KEY IN SEALING MAN IS AN OVERBEARING HOPE OR APPETITE TO SEE LOVE, WE MUST NOT TRANSGRESS THE CONVICTIONS OF OBEDIENCE TO GOD WHEN WE GET THEM LEST WE HINDER OURSELVES AND BE DESTROYED!

EASY TO BE SAVED, HARD TO BE LOST

THE DOCTRINE OF SANCTIFICATION TEACHES US THAT IT IS *EASY* TO BE SAVED AND *HARD* TO BE LOST! WHEN ONE UNDERSTANDS THE TRUE PROCESSES THAT OPERATE IN SANCTIFICATION, WE COME AROUND TO RECOGNIZE THAT WE, BY OUR INDECISIVENESS, OR BY CHERISHING SOME HIDDEN OR OCCASIONAL LOVE FOR SELF, HINDER OUR SANCTIFICATION! WE FIND IT HARD TO BE SAVED BECAUSE WE FIND OURSELVES TOO DISOBEDIENT TO GOD'S GRACIOUS LOVE. WE NEED TO KEEP OUR EYES ON THAT SANCTIFYING LOVE AND IT WILL CERTAINLY DO ITS WORK OF BRINGING US TO *SEALED PERFECTION* AS CERTAIN AS IT DID TO ENOCH AND OTHER MEN OF OLD! IT IS GOD THAT SANCTIFIES US BY OUR CO-OPERATION THAT HE ENLISTS. THUS SANCTIFICATION IS *SYNERGISTIC* AND IS A *SURETY* IF WE DO OUR PART WHICH IS SO EASY! HOW HARD IS IT TO FIGHT AGAINST GOD, AND HOW EASY IT IS JUST TO SUBMIT ONESELF TO HIM!

I AM CONVINCED THAT THEY WHO REALLY LOVE RIGHTEOUSNESS AND HATE INIQUITY SHALL FIND NO DIFFICULTY IN THEIR SANCTIFICATION! FOR US TO BE SAVED IS AN EASY MATTER, FOR US TO BE LOST RENDERS IT DIFFICULT TO HIDE FROM LOVE WHEN IT IS PERSISTENT AND EVER PRESENT!

FOUR DIFFERENT STAGES IN SANCTIFICATION

SANCTIFICATION HAS FOUR DIFFERENT STAGES, THREE OF WHICH INTERLAP SO THAT AS THE THIRD STAGE COMES, IT IS A PERMANIZING OF THE FIRST TWO! THE FOURTH STAGE IS A SETTLING INTO THE THIRD! THESE FOUR STAGES ARE: *LINGERING VICTORY, CONQUERING VICTORY, ACHIEVED VICTORY* AND *SEALED PERFECTION!* LINGERING VICTORY, THE FIRST OF THE FOUR, IS THE GENESIS EXPERIENCE OF THOSE WHO JUST ACCEPTED CHRIST AND ARE BABES! THOUGH THEY MAY HAVE GOTTEN SOME MINUTE MEASURE OF CONQUERING VICTORY AS THEY JUST EMBRACED CHRIST, NEVERTHELESS, THE REAL CONQUERING VICTORY BEGINS AS THEY BEGIN TO DEAL WITH THEIR FAULTS BY FAITH! UNDER *LINGERING VICTORY*, CHRIST ONLY ABIDES IN THE HEART AS THEY ABIDE IN HIM BY HEARING PREACHING, DISCUSSING SOME PORTION OF TRUTH OR BY STUDYING TRUTH, BUT CHRIST HAS NOT YET BEEN APPROACHED AS A SAVIOUR FROM PERSONAL SINS, THUS CONQUERING VICTORY IS NOT REALLY KNOWN EXPERIENTIALLY!

ONE IN THIS CONDITION COULD BE SAVED ESPECIALLY IF THEY DIE AS A MARTYR, BUT THEY ARE HARDLY ABLE TO TAKE ON TEMPTATION AND OVERCOME THEM, THOUGH THEY CAN ABIDE IN SOME TRUTH WHILE TEMPTATION IS BEING PROSECUTED, WHICH TEMPTATION THEY IGNORE!

IN *CONQUERING VICTORY*, THE PERSON TAKES THE PARTICULAR SIN OR TEMPTATION WITHOUT FALLING INTO IT, OR HOLDING IT IN THE PRESENT CONSCIOUSNESS AS PLEASURABLE OR AS LOVE, AND THEY MATCH THE TRUTH OF GOD'S RESPLENDENT LOVE WITH THE SIN, THUS EXPOSING ITS CONTRADICTIONS AND DESTROYING THE DECEPTIONS OF IT, UNTIL IT HAS NOT THE SLIGHTEST APPEAL AS IT ONCE HAD IN THE DECEPTIVE FORM IT WAS PRESENTED! WHEN THIS HAS SUFFICIENTLY TRANSPIRED ABOUT A PARTICULAR SIN, THIS IS CONQUERING VICTORY! WE SHOULD BE USING OUR TIME WITH THOUGHTS OF OVERCOMING SIN THAT WE SHOULD *QUICKLY* REACH *ACHIEVED VICTORY!* THIS THIRD STAGE IS THE POSITION WHERE WE HAVE DEALT FAITHFULLY WITH ALL OUR *CULTURED AND INHERITED TENDENCIES* TO SIN, WHERE WE HAVE ZEROED IN ON THE SUBCONSCIOUS GENESIS OF ALL IMPULSIVE SINS, WHERE WE HAVE WHOLISTIC TRUTHS THAT CAN EACH DEAL WITH MANY TEMPTATIONS, WHERE WE SEE AND TRAVEL IN OUR PATH OF REVEALED DUTY IN THE *PLAN OF ATONEMENT,* FULFILLING ALL GOD GIVEN DUTIES, THUS WE HAVE NO MORE SINS TO DEAL WITH! THE GENERAL AND MINUTE PRINCIPLES OF SIN MUST ALL BE UNDERSTOOD AND WE MUST BE SO SOBER MINDED AS TO ALWAYS DISCERN THE ENEMY COMING WITH ONE OF THESE EVIL PRINCIPLES, AND WE HAVE GRACE TO DEAL WITH ALL EXPERIENTIALLY!

WHEN WE ARE GIVEN THE TRUTHS OF THE LATTER RAIN THAT SETTLE US INTO ACHIEVED VICTORY, THIS IS *SEALED PERFECTION!* UNDER THE FOURTH STAGE THE APPETITE OF HOPE HAS REACHED AN UNBREAKABLE STATE, AND THE FAITH IS THE *SEVEN VIEWS* OF THE ATONEMENT IN *ONE WHOLE* AS THE HEART SEES AND ACCEPTS CLEAR MAPPED OUT DUTY!

TEXTUAL RATIFICATION

1. **RIGTEOUSNESS BY FAITH INCLUDES SANCTIFICATION**
   (ROMANS 5:9; HEBREWS 13:12); 1 PETER 1:7-9; COLOSSIANS 2:6,7; 2 TIMOTHY 1:13; PHILIPPIANS 3:9; (ROMANS 5:1; PHILIPPIANS 4:7).

2. **SANCTIFICATION IS THE MAINTAINANCE OF RIGHTEOUSNESS IN THE SOUL.**
   1 JOHN 3:7; ISAIAH 54:17; ROMANS 5:21,5; ROMANS 8:4; ROMANS 6:11-13,16,18,19,23; 1 CORINTHIANS 1:30; GALATIANS 5:5,22,25; EPHESIANS 3:17; EPHESIANS 5:8-11; COLOSSIANS 2:6,7; 1 TIMOTHY 6:11; 2 TIMOTHY 4:7.

3. **SANCTIFICATION IS UNBROKEN REPENTANCE, BELIEVE, IMPUTATION.**
   TITUS 2:14; HEBREWS 10:39; 1 PETER 1:8.

4. **DEVELOPMENT, MATURING OF FAITH AND GOOD WORKS (CULTURING AFFECTIONS IN A SPIRITUAL CONTEXT).** 1THESSALONIANS 4:3-9; 2 PETER 3:17,18; **WORKS:** COLOSSIANS 3:17; 2 THESSALONIANS 3:13; TITUS 3:8; HEBREWS 13:20,21; JAMES 3:13; **AFFECTIONS:** EPHESIANS 4:32; PHILIPPIANS 4:8; COLOSSIANS 3:1,2,12-14.

5. **SANCTIFICATION WITHIN THE STATE OF SINFREENESS.**
   PHILIPPIANS 3:15; 1 JOHN 3:9,2; COLOSSIANS 2:10; 2 TIMOTHY 1:13; 1 THESSALONIANS 2:13; 1 THESSALONIANS 3:12,13; 2 THESSALONIANS 3:3; HEBREWS 12:23; JAMES 3:10-13; 1 PETER 1:22.

6. **SANCTIFICATION MADE REAL BY HOPE.**
   COLOSSIANS 1:23; 1 THESSALONIANS 1:3; 1 THESSALONIANS 5:8; 2 THESSALONIANS 2:16,17; TITUS 3:7; 1 PETER 1:13; MATTHEW 5:6; JOHN 7:17; ROMANS 8:24,25; ROMANS 5:5; 1 JOHN 3:3; ROMANS 15:4; 1 PETER 3:15.

7. **DIFFERENT STAGES IN SANCTIFICATION.**
   THE FOUR STAGES IN SANCTIFICATION.

A. **LINGERING VICTORY (BY ABIDING)**
   2 JOHN 9; 1 JOHN 3:6; PSALM 18:17,18; 1 SAMUEL 26:3; PSALM 91:1; 1 CORINTHIANS 7:20,24.

B. **CONQUERING VICTORY - USING FAITH AND LOVE TO NEGATE THE EFFECTIVENESS OF SINFUL VALUES.** PHILIPPIANS 3:9-16; 1 JOHN 3:3; EPHESIANS 4:25-32; EPHESIANS 5:3-5; HEBREWS 12:1,4; JOHN 15:4-6; 1 JOHN 2:27,28; JAMES 1:2-4,21.

C. **ACHIEVED VICTORY - NO PERSONAL, INHERENT OR PRONE FAULT TO DEAL WITH, ALL OVERCOME BY FAITH AND LOVE.** 1THESSALONIANS 3:12,13; PHILIPPIANS 3:12; 1 JOHN 2:14; JAMES 1:12; 1 PETER 1:7.

D. **SEALED PERFECTION - LATTER RAIN GRACES SETTLES MAN INTO ACHIEVED VICTORY, CAN'T FALL BACK.** REVELATION 7:3,4; REVELATION 14:1-5; REVELATION 15:2-4; EZEKIEL 9:4.

8. **EASY TO BE SAVED, HARD TO BE LOST.**
   1 THESSALONIANS 5:23,24; 1 PETER 1:15,16; ACTS 9:5; ROMANS 5:20.

9. **UNBROKEN COMMUNION OF MEDITATION.**
   EPHESIANS 6:18; PHILIPPIANS 4:6; COLOSSIANS 4:2; 1 THESSALONIANS 5:17.

10. **THEOLOGICAL VIEW OF MAN IN THE STATE OF SEALED PERFECTION.**
    REVELATION 14:1,3; REVELATION 15:3,4; EXODUS 15:1-21.

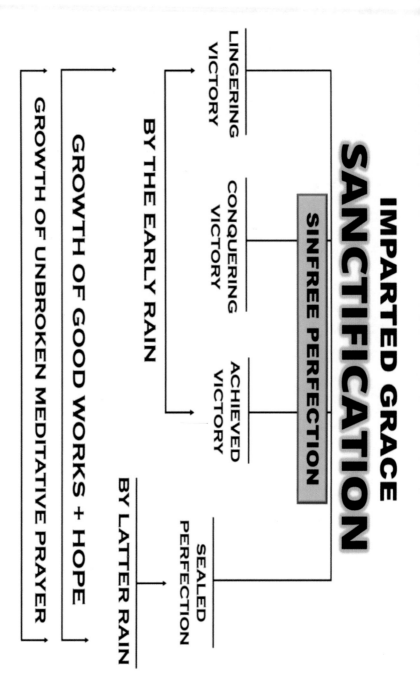

SANCTIFICATION

IMPARTED GRACE

SINFREE PERFECTION

LINGERING VICTORY

CONQUERING VICTORY

ACHIEVED VICTORY

SEALED PERFECTION

BY THE EARLY RAIN

BY LATTER RAIN

GROWTH OF GOOD WORKS + HOPE

GROWTH OF UNBROKEN MEDITATIVE PRAYER

SANCTIFICATION IS SYNERGISTIC!

PREPARED AND PUBLISHED BY THE SERVICES OF THUSIA (SDA). FEBRUARY, 1986.

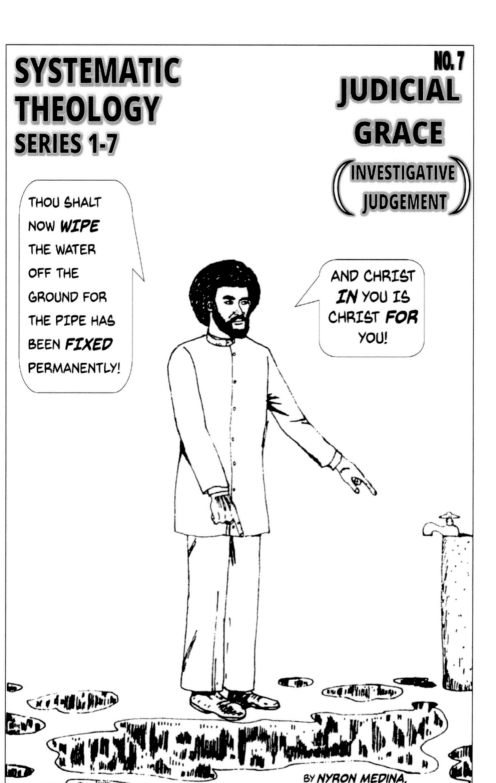

A COURSE IN SYSTEMATIC THEOLOGY

PILLAR SEVEN : ## INVESTIGATIVE JUDGEMENT (*JUDICIAL GRACE*)

THE SEVENTH AND FINAL PILLAR OF SYSTEMATIC THEOLOGY, WHICH IS THE FIFTH POINT OF THE ATONEMENT IS CALLED *JUDICIAL GRACE, THE INVESTIGATIVE JUDGEMENT* OR THE *BLOTTING OUT OF SINS;* IT IS ALSO CALLED *THE CLEANSING OF THE HEAVENLY SANCTUARY!* THIS IS THE UNIQUE CONTRIBUTION OF SEVENTH-DAY ADVENTISM TO CHRISTIAN THEOLOGY AS DISCOVERED AND DEVELOPED BY THE REFORMATION; THIS IS THE FINAL PART OF THE *PROTESTANT REFORMATION!* THE GOSPEL WAS REVEALED TO BE A WHOLE TRAIN, PARTS OF THE CARRIAGES WERE REMOVED THROUGH THE LONG CENTURIES OF PAPAL SUPREMACY UNTIL ALMOST THE WHOLE TRAIN HAD DISAPPEARED, BUT AT THE OPENING OF THE REFORMATION GOD USED MEN TO RESTORE THE CARRIAGES, AND THIS RESTORATION HAD CONTINUED UNTIL THE FINAL CARRIAGE HAS BEEN FULLY RESTORED.

NOW THE TRAIN IS HEADING HOME, AND ALL THE NECESSARY DWELLING PLACES FOR THOSE WHO CHOOSE THE *ATONEMENT* HAVE BEEN PROVIDED SO THAT THEY CAN RIDE AND REACH HOME IN SAFETY! THIS IS THE END, AND THE FINAL CARRIAGE WHICH THE WORLD VIEWS AS IT HEADS HOME IS THE MESSAGE FOR THIS TIME; GOD WILL *HIDE* A MULTITUDE OF SHAMEFUL SINS BY THE *JUDICIAL GRACE* OF CHRIST TO THOSE WHO ARE *JUSTIFIED* AND *SANCTIFIED* BY THE IMPUTED FAITH AND RIGHTEOUSNESS OF JESUS CHRIST! THUS, THE ISSUE WAS NOT WHAT HORRIBLE AND OBFUSCACIOUS SINS MEN HAVE COMMITTED, BUT IN WHOM DO THEY TRUST THAT THEY MIGHT BE *TWICE* JUSTIFIED, OR THAT THEY MIGHT RECEIVE THE *LEGAL TRANSACTION*, FOR ITS CONTINUATION, FOR *THE POST LEGAL TRANSACTION*. WOULD MEN RECEIVE THE *INCHRISTMENT* FOR THE *BLOTTING OUT*? WOULD THEY RECEIVE *INNER* CLEANSING FOR *OUTER* CLEANSING?

THE PATTERN OF GOD IN DEALING WITH SIN

THE PLAN OF SALVATION OR ATONEMENT STARTS OFF WITH *GOD*, PROVIDING BY HIS *LOVE*, THE *INCARNATION*, THE *SINLESS LIFE* OF CHRIST, THE *SACRIFICIAL CRUCIFIXION*, THE *RESURRECTION* AND *THE ANOINTING OF CHRIST AS THE HIGH PRIEST!* IT IS ALSO MADE UP OF *PREVENIENT GRACE* (THE CALLING), *RENEWING GRACE* (JUSTIFICATION), *IMPARTED GRACE* (SANCTIFICATION) AND *JUDICIAL GRACE* (INVESTIGATIVE JUDGEMENT)! IT IS THE LOVE OF GOD SHINING IN THE FACE OF CHRIST WHO IS THE PLAN OF ATONEMENT THAT CONVICTS MAN OF SIN, RIGHTEOUSNESS AND OF JUDGEMENT, AND THIS IS THE WORK OF PREVENIENT GRACE! NOW IF THE MAN REPENTS AND BELIEVES, WHAT HE IS FORGIVEN OF IS SIN *IN HIS HEART* OR THE *CARNAL MIND!* GOD DOES NOT IMPUTE THE CARNAL MIND UNTO HIM AND THE DIVINE MIND IS IMPUTED UNTO HIM, THUS HE *IS MADE RIGHTEOUS* SUBJECTIVELY. THIS IS RENEWING GRACE, AND IT CONTINUES IN UNBROKEN SEQUENCE AS IMPARTED GRACE OR SANCTIFICATION!

BUT, SEEING THAT THE DEFECT IN THE HEART HAS BEEN TAKEN CARE OF BY *JUSTIFICATION*, WHAT IS IT THAT TAKES CARE OF ALL THE *PAST SINS*? IF GOD WERE TO REMOVE ALL THE PAST SINS FIRST, CASTING THEM INTO THE DEPTHS OF THE SEA AND REMEMBERING THEM NO MORE (SO TO SPEAK), AND AFTER THE MAN IS FAITHFUL FOR A TERM, HE FALLS BACK INTO SIN AND DIES A LOST SOUL, WHAT SHALL BECOME OF ALL THE PAST SINS WHICH HE WAS FORGIVEN OF? IS HE STILL FORGIVEN FOR THEM? IS CHRIST THE SAVIOUR OF A LOST MAN? HOW WOULD GOD REMEMBER THEM IF HE PROMISES TO REMEMBER THEM NO MORE? HOW WOULD HE RECALL THEM WITHOUT GOING AGAINST HIS OWN WORD?

I

IT IS ONLY OBVIOUS, THAT THE SYMBOL OF CASTING SINS INTO THE SEA AND REMEMBERING THEM NO MORE, WHICH IS THE FORGIVENESS OF SINS THAT ARE PAST, OR REMOVING THEM FROM MAN'S RESPONSIBILITY, DOES NOT TAKE PLACE AT THE JUSTIFICATION OF THE MAN! JUSTIFICATION TAKES CARE OF SIN *IN* THE MAN, HIS CARNAL MIND, NOT HIS PAST SINS, THEN HE IS GRANTED A PERIOD OF PROBATION FOR SANCTIFICATION! AND IF HE IS *FAITHFUL* TO THIS SUBJECTIVE WORK, IF HE OVERCOMES ALL HIS SINS OR DIES IN THE PROCESS, HIS NAME IMMEDIATELY COMES UP BEFORE GOD IN THE *JUDGEMENT*, AND HIS GUILT FOR THESE PAST SINS IS *ABSOLVED* BECAUSE OF *CHRIST'S RIGHTEOUSNESS IN* HIM. HE IS NO LONGER COUNTED RESPONSIBLE FOR THEM BECAUSE GOD'S LOVE IS IN HIM. SO THUS HIS PAST SINS ARE BLOTTED OUT (SO TO SPEAK), OR HE IS FORGIVEN FOR ALL HIS PAST SINS! IT IS OBVIOUSLY SEEN IN THIS SIMPLE ILLUSTRATION, THAT IF A PIPE IS BROKEN, DO WE WIPE UP THE SPILT WATER FIRST, AND THEN FIX THE PIPE? OR IS IT NOT REASONABLE TO SAY THAT THE PIPE SHOULD BE FIXED FIRST, AND THEN, IF THAT HAPPENS, ONLY THEN THE SPILT WATER SHOULD BE BLOTTED UP! EVEN SO, GOD MUST DEAL WITH SIN *IN US FIRST*, HE MUST FIX US BY SUBSTITUTING THE CARNAL MIND SUBJECTIVELY WITH THE DIVINE MIND FIRST. THEN HE CAN BLOT OUT ALL OUR PAST SINS FROM OUR RESPONSIBILITY ON THE BASIS OF OUR BEING REFORMED!

WHAT IS JUDICIAL GRACE?

JUDICIAL GRACE IS THAT ACT OF GOD IN WHICH HE ABSOLVES THE FINALLY PENITENT OF GUILT OR RESPONSIBILITY FOR ALL PAST SINS ON THE BASIS OF BEING REFORMED BY THE ABIDING PRESENCE OF THE DIVINE NATURE OR SPIRITUAL LAW, EITHER BY DYING IN CHRIST ON THE ROAD OF SANCTIFICATION OR BY OVERCOMING ALL SIN AND REACHING THE STATE OF *SEALED PERFECTION*. IN THE MAN'S HEART IS THE LOVE OF GOD OR HIS RIGHTEOUSNESS AS THE MAN'S VALUE, AND AS GOD SEES THIS IN THE JUDGEMENT THE PAST SINS ARE REMOVED, THUS THE MAN IS GLORIFIED AS A THOROUGHLY REDEEMED BEING! BUT THAT IS NOT ALL! IT WAS SATAN THAT TEMPTED THE MAN TO COMMIT ALL HIS SINS, AND THE MAN WAS BORN TOTALLY DEPRAVED OR IN A STATE OF DISADVANTAGE HENCE WITH NO SECURITY FROM SATAN WHO TOOK ADVANTAGE OF HIM. CALLED BY GOD AND JUSTIFIED WHEN HE RESPONDED, AND CONTINUED FAITHFULLY SANCTIFIED, HE PROVED THAT IF HE HAD CHANCE (WHICH HE DID HAVE IN THE PLAN OF *ATONEMENT*) HE WOULD HAVE REJECTED SATAN'S DOMINION OVER HIM, FOR, BEHOLD, HE HAS REJECTED THIS EXCRUCIATING DOMINION. HE IS THEREFORE *NOT RESPONSIBLE* FOR ALL THE SINS HE COMMITTED! WHO IS THEREFORE RESPONSIBLE? IT IS SATAN WHO CAUSED HIM TO COMMIT THEM! SATAN MUST THEREFORE EXPERIENCE THE RESULTS OF THIS RESPONSIBILITY; HE MUST EXPERIENCE RETRIBUTION FOR BEING THE INSTIGATOR OR ENCOURAGER. THUS, IN THE *MILLENNIUM* SATAN IS GIVEN CONSCIOUSNESS OF THIS RESPONSIBILITY, AND AFTER THE MILLENNIUM HE PERISHES FOR THIS ALSO. THIS CONCLUDES THE ATONEMENT!

THIS ROLE OF SCAPEGOAT THAT SATAN IS MADE TO FULFIL IS NOT AN ACT OF SAVING MAN FROM SIN, BECAUSE WHERE THERE IS NO SHEDDING OF BLOOD THERE IS NO REMISSION. IN OTHER WORDS, SATAN DOES NOT GIVE HIS LIFE TO SUBJECTIVELY DELIVER US FROM SIN, SO HE IS NOT OUR SAVIOUR! RATHER, THE SCAPEGOAT PART OF THE ATONEMENT IS CALLED *"POST-REDEMPTIVE-SUBSTANTIATORY."* WHAT DOES THAT MEAN? WELL HERE IS THE EXPLANATION:

A. IT HAPPENS AFTER THE SUBJECTIVE AND OBJECTIVE REDEMPTION OF THE SAINTS, BUT IS YET A SUBSTANTIATING NECESSITY OF THE ATONEMENT THAT HINGES ON ITS EDGE!

B. ITS PURPOSE IS TO, BY JUST ATTRIBUTION, RATIFY THE WORK OF ABSOLVING OF THE GUILT AND RANSOMING FROM CONDEMNATION THAT JUST OCCURRED WITH THE SAINTS! THUS, THE SAINTS ARE GLORIFIED AND THE WORK OF ATONEMENT IS SEEN TO BE ABSOLUTELY COMPLETE INDEED! THIS IS AN ILLUSTRATION: A HOUSE MAY BE ALREADY CLEANED AND FURNISHED AND THOROUGHLY PUT AWAY, ALL THE RUBBISH IS ALREADY OUTSIDE OF THE HOUSE AND IS NO LONGER ATTRIBUTED TO IT, ALL THAT IS NOW LEFT TO DO, IS TO THROW THE RUBBISH INTO FIRE TO BE CONSUMED! WHILE THE HOUSE IS ALREADY THOROUGHLY CLEANED, YET THROWING THE RUBBISH INTO THE FIRE TO BE CONSUMED IS YET A PART OF THE TASK OF CLEANING THE HOUSE, ALTHOUGH THIS WORK DOES NOT ITSELF CLEAN THE HOUSE! IT IS A POST-CLEANSING SUBSTANTIATING WORK, A WORK THAT SUBSTANTIATES THE WORK OF CLEANSING THAT HAS BEEN COMPLETED. SO IT IS WITH THE SCAPEGOAT!

C. WITH THE SAINTS, GUILT IS ABSOLVED! THIS MEANS THAT RESPONSIBILITY FOR PAST SINS IS NO LONGER IMPUTED TO THEM BY GOD BECAUSE OF PRESENT SUBJECTIVE AND ACCEPTED *INNOCENCE* WHICH IS THE INSHOWING OF RIGHTEOUSNESS. THIS IS GOD'S GRACIOUSNESS TO WHICH IS ADDED THE BLOTTING OUT OF ALL PAST SINS, AND THIS IS FREEING THE MAN FROM THE CONDEMNATION FOR ALL HIS PAST SINS!

GOD'S HOLINESS WITHIN, WHEN CLUNG TO (UNDER SANCTIFICATION) AS THE MAN'S PERSONAL RIGHTEOUSNESS, VINDICATES THE MAN'S INTENTIONS TO HOLINESS MAKING HIM SUBJECTIVELY INNOCENT. THUS GOD, BY HIS OWN ESTIMATION, DECLARES THE MAN INNOCENT, AND THIS ABSOLVES HIM FROM GUILT! THE CONSEQUENTIAL SUFFERINGS AND DEATH FOR ALL HORRIBLE SINS, THAT CHRIST EXPERIENCED, WHEN UNDERSTOOD, GIVES REPENTANCE TO THE MAN FOR HIS SUBJECTIVE JUSTIFICATION. THE MAN'S DEPTH OF CHOICE, THUS DISPLAY OF INTENTION, DECLARES HIS INNOCENCE IN THE WHOLE MATTER OF HIS TRANSGRESSIONS, THAT GIVEN THE CHOICE HE WOULD NOT HAVE SINNED BUT FOR THE FACT THAT HE WAS BORN IN SIN AND MISLED BEFORE CONVERSION! WHO THEN IS RESPONSIBLE FOR HIS SINS? IT IS SATAN, WHO IN THE FIRST PLACE TEMPTED HIM TO COMMIT THEM, THUS SATAN IS GUILTY FOR THE MAN'S SINS! THIS GUILT IS PLACED IN SATAN'S CONSCIOUSNESS DURING THE MILLENNIUM FOR WHICH HE IS ALSO DESTROYED AFTER THE MILLENNIUM! IN THIS, IT IS SEEN THAT THE HORRIBLE SUFFERINGS OF CHRIST WERE NOT PENALTY FOR SATAN'S RESPONSIBILITY AND CONDEMNATION FOR THE SINS OF THE SAINTS; THEY WERE FOR THE SINS OF THE SAINTS! THE MATTER OF THE SCAPEGOAT IS PARTICULARLY THE COMPLETION OF THE FORGIVENESS OF SINS FOR THE VINDICATION OF GOD!

III

IT HAS BEEN SAID BY SOME THAT AN INVESTIGATIVE JUDGEMENT IS NOT A NECESSITY, THAT THIS IS AN ADDITION TO THE GOSPEL OF CHRIST AND IT TAKES AWAY FROM THE FINISHED WORK! BUT WHILE THIS *SYSTEMATIC THEOLOGY SERIES* IN NO WAY WAS AN APOLOGETIC DISSERTATION, YET ITS DEFINITE ASSERTIONS AND THE FACT THAT IT IS BIBLICALLY BASED WAS A DEFEAT TO ANY CHALLENGE FROM THE FALSE APOSTATE EVANGELICALS THEOLOGY OR CATHOLIC THEOLOGY! ALSO INCLUDED IN THIS GREAT AFFIRMATION OF THEOLOGY IS THE DOCTRINE OF *INVESTIGATIVE JUDGEMENT!* FAR FROM IT, THIS IS IN NO WAY AN IMPEDIMENT TO THE GOSPEL, BUT IT IS THE REVELATION OF THE FINAL PART OF THE WHOLE, GREAT, GRAND ATONEMENT RETURNED TO THE EARTH FROM THE GRACIOUS LIGHT NOW SHINING FROM THE SECOND APARTMENT OF THE TRUE AND REAL HEAVENLY SANCTUARY. (REVELATION 11:19, REVELATION 14:6,7; HEBREWS 8:2, HEBREWS 9:11, HEBREWS 10:21; REVELATION 14:17,18; REVELATION 15:5,6). IN THE HOLY SCRIPTURES, THE WORK OF SALVATION IS DESCRIBED AS *JUDGEMENT.* (DEUTERONOMY 1:17; DEUTERONOMY 32:4; PSALM 37:28; PSALM 97:2; ISAIAH 33:22; PSALM 9:1,4,5,7,8; PROVERBS 20:8; DEUTERONOMY 32:36; PSALM 35:23,24; ISAIAH 1:27; JOHN 12:28-32; JOHN 16:8,11; JOHN 3:14-21; JOHN 9:35-39.), AND INVESTIGATION IS ALSO TAUGHT IN THE SCRIPTURES, (GENESIS 3:9,11; GENESIS 11:5; JEREMIAH 17:10; ZEPHANIAH 1:12; ROMANS 8:27.)! THIS INVESTIGATION IS GOD SEARCHING OR VIEWING, AS HE MUST VIEW THE WHOLE CHARACTER OF THE MAN IN HIS OWN MIND!

THE FINAL PART OF THE PLAN OF SALVATION WHICH IS THE MAKING UP OF THE SUBJECTS OF GOD'S KINGDOM (DANIEL 2:34,35,44,45) NECESSITATES A REVIEW OF THE CHARACTER OF GOD'S SUBJECTS, NOT IN THE TIME-CONSUMING SENSE AS IS REQUIRED BY FRAIL HUMAN BEINGS, BUT MERELY AS GOD KNOWING WHO HAS BEEN FAITHFUL AND WHO HAS NOT BEEN, AND GRANTING *JUDICIAL GRACE* TO THOSE WHO CLING TO INNOCENCE IN THEIR HEARTS AND REVEALED IN THEIR WORKS (EZEKIEL 18:5-9,21,22,27,28; ROMANS 3:25; 1 JOHN 4:17)!

THE NECESSITY OF THE INVESTIGATIVE JUDGEMENT IS BASED UPON THE PERFECTION OF GOD'S DIVINE NATURE OF LOVE WHICH OBVIOUSLY BRINGS FORTH PERFECT ACTS IN HIS DEALING WITH SIN, THUS A PERFECTLY STRUCTURED PLAN OF ATONEMENT! THE PERFECT STRUCTURE OF PROVIDENTIAL GRACE MUST PORTRAY THAT PERFECT APPLICATION IS NECESSARY THAT THE PLAN WILL BE SUCCESSFUL IN SAVING MEN (DEUTERONOMY 32:3,4; PSALM 18:30); AND AFTER THE CALLING AND JUSTIFICATION, A PERIOD OF *PROBATION* WAS NECESSARY FOR SANCTIFICATION, SO THAT ONLY IF THE MAN WAS TRULY REFORMED, HIS PAST SINS WERE TO BE BLOTTED OUT, HENCE THE NEED FOR THE JUDGEMENT! THE FACT THAT THE PAST SINS ARE NOT BLOTTED OUT AT CONVERSION IS TESTIFIED TO IN THE SCRIPTURES (ACTS 3:19)! THAT WHICH IS FIRST DEALT WITH IS THE PURGING OF THE MIND (EZEKIEL 18:31; PSALM 51:6,7,10) AND ACCORDING TO THE SUCCESS OF THE WORK ACCOMPLISHED WITHIN, THEN THE MAN IS FORGIVEN FOR PAST SINS (1 JOHN 4:17; ROMANS 2:6,7,13,16; ROMANS 3:25; MATTHEW 10:22)! THUS, THE INVESTIGATIVE JUDGEMENT IS NOT AN IMPEDIMENT TO THE GOSPEL, IT IS THE GOSPEL ITSELF (REVELATION14:6,7), FOR IT IS THE FINAL PART OF THE APPLICATION OF THE WORK FINISHED AT THE CROSS, AT THE RESURRECTION AND ANOINTING WHICH IS CALLED PROVIDENTIAL GRACE! THE WORK OF INVESTIGATIVE JUDGEMENT IS THE WORK OF GOD FORGIVING US FOR ALL OUR PAST SINS ON THE CRITERION OF *DYING* ON THE PATH OF SANCTIFICATION OR ON THE BASIS OF REACHING *SEALED PERFECTION* AS IS NECESSARY OF THE 144,000! AT JUSTIFICATION, THE MAN WHO REPENTED AND BELIEVED IS MADE RIGHTEOUS, MADE INNOCENT IN CHARACTER AND INTENTIONS, BUT THAT WHICH IS MAINTAINED IN SANCTIFICATION DOES NOT TAKE CARE OF GUILT FOR PAST SINS OR FOR CONDEMNATION OF THEM!

THE WORK ON THE CROSS MAKES AVAILABLE *LIFE* FOR THE *INCHRISTMENT,* AND BY WAY OF INNER CHANGE, FINALLY DELIVERS FROM CONDEMNATION! BUT WHEREAS GUILT IS ABSOLVED BECAUSE OF THE INCHRISTMENT, GUILT FOR OUR GUILT (AS WE ARE MADE INNOCENT) IS FULLY CHARGED UPON SATAN THE SCAPEGOAT WHO PERISHES FOR THIS!

HOW ARE OUR SINS CARRIED INTO THE SANCTUARY?

THIS EVENT IS TO BE UNDERSTOOD BY TAKING MANY THINGS INTO CONSIDERATION! IT IS KNOWN THAT CHRIST ASCENDED INTO HEAVEN INTO THE FIRST APARTMENT OF THE HEAVENLY SANCTUARY (HEBREWS 6:19,20; HEBREWS 8:1,2; HEBREWS 9:11,12,24; HEBREWS 10:21). IN 1844 HE ENTERED INTO THE SECOND APARTMENT TO CONCLUDE THE WHOLE, GREAT, GRAND WORK OF ATONEMENT (DANIEL 8:14; REVELATION 11:19; MALACHI 3:1; DANIEL 7:10)! WHEN A SINNER REPENTS, BELIEVES AND IS JUSTIFIED, HIS NAME IS IMMEDIATELY WRITTEN IN THE **LAMB'S BOOK OF LIFE** (LUKE 10:20; REVELATION 20:12; REVELATION 21:27), THERE IS ALSO A **BOOK OF REMEMBRANCE** THAT IS PREPARED BEFORE THE LORD IN WHICH IS RECORDED THE GOOD DEEDS OR GOOD CHARACTER THAT THE CONVERTED MAN DEVELOPS EVERY MOMENT (MALACHI 3:16; PSALM 56:8; NEHEMIAH 13:14)! THERE IS ALSO A BOOK THAT RECORDS ALL THE EVIL DEEDS OF THE MAN (REVELATION 20:12,13)! HOWEVER, AS HE REPENTS DAILY ON THE ROAD OF SANCTIFICATION AND CONFESSES HIS SINS, THEY ARE RECORDED AS CONFESSED AND FORSAKEN SINS! BUT HOW DO THESE SINS ENTER INTO THE HEAVENLY SANCTUARY? WELL, THROUGH THE **BLOOD** OF CHRIST! WHEN THE ANCIENT JEWISH PRIEST DAILY TOOK THE BLOOD OF THE SLAIN LAMB AND SPRINKLED IT ON THE VAIL OF THE EARTHLY SANCTUARY (LEVITICUS 4:6,17), THIS SHOWED THAT OUR SINS WERE IN ANTI-TYPE TO BE CARRIED INTO THE HEAVENLY SANCTUARY IN THE FORM OF HOW WE CONFESSED THEM! IF THEY WERE JUST ACKNOWLEDGED AS A WRONG, THIS IS NOT A SIGN OF TRUE REPENTANCE; IT IS THE FALSE ONE, MERE REMORSE AS WAS DONE BY JUDAS WHO KILLED HIMSELF (MATTHEW 27:3-5)! IN TRUE CONFESSION, THE NATURE AND WRONG OF THE SIN WERE TO BE UNDERSTOOD AS THE SPIRIT GAVE WITNESS, AND THEY WERE TO BE ACKNOWLEDGED OR CONFESSED BEFORE GOD IN THE LIGHT OF THE TRUTHS OF THE PLAN OF ATONEMENT!

SO THAT WHEN CONFESSED, THE SIN, EXPRESSED IN THE LIGHT OF THE PLAN OF SALVATION WAS SO RECORDED AS A CONFESSED AND FORSAKEN SIN. THESE ARE THE PAST SINS THAT ARE TO BE BLOTTED FROM THE RESPONSIBILITY OF THE SAINTS!

ALSO, THE PRIEST CARRYING THE BLOOD INTO THE SANCTUARY OR EATING THE FLESH OF THE SLAIN LAMB IN THE FIRST APARTMENT OF THE SANCTUARY, SYMBOLIZED, THAT OUR SINS ENTERED THERE RECORDED IN THE LIGHT OF THE TRUTHS THAT CHRIST, WHO THE PRIEST SYMBOLIZED, IS (LEVITICUS 4:5,16; LEVITICUS 10:13,17,18)! THIS IS HOW OUR SINS ARE CARRIED INTO THE HEAVENLY SANCTUARY! THE CLEANSING OF THE HEAVENLY SANCTUARY IS NOT THE REMOVING OF A LITERAL POLLUTION IN THAT SANCTUARY, BUT IT IS THE FORENSIC WORK THAT AFFECTS OUR STANDING WITH GOD (LEVITICUS 16:19,20; 1 JOHN 4:17; HEBREWS 3:14)! WHEN THE NAME OF THE CONVERTED COMES UP BEFORE GOD AT DEATH (HEBREWS 9:27; REVELATION 20:12), OR IN THE TIME WHEN THE LIVING SAINTS ARE SEALED, THE BOOKS ARE INVESTIGATED! THE BOOK OF REMEMBRANCE WITH THE RECORDS OF HIS CHARACTER IS SEARCHED, THE BOOK OF INIQUITY WITH THE ACCOUNTS OF RECORDED SINS THAT ARE TRULY CONFESSED OR UNCONFESSED IS ALSO SEARCHED. (REVELATION 20:12,13; DANIEL 7:10). AND IF THE MAN DIED ON THE WAY OF SANCTIFICATION IN A CONVERTED STATE, OR IF ALL SINS ARE THOROUGHLY CONFESSED AND FORSAKEN WITH BLOOD, IN THE CASE OF THE LIVING SEALED SAINTS, THOSE SINS ARE THEREFORE REMOVED FROM THEIR RESPONSIBILITY OR BLOTTED OUT (ACTS 3:19; ISAIAH 43:25)!

IF THEY HAVE UNCONFESSED AND UNFORSAKEN SINS ON THE BOOKS, THESE STAND AGAINST THEM, AND THEIR NAMES ARE REMOVED FROM THE LAMB'S BOOK OF LIFE! THIS IS THE FINAL WORK OF THE ATONEMENT THAT SAVES US FROM ALL PAST SINS AND MAKES UP THE SUBJECTS OF GOD'S KINGDOM (DANIEL 2:44, MATTHEW 22:14; REVELATION 17:14)!

THE INVESTIGATIVE JUDGEMENT IN NATURAL AND HISTORICAL THEOLOGY

SOME DOUBTERS OF THE INVESTIGATIVE JUDGEMENT WHO SHALL NOT BENEFIT FROM THIS JUDICIAL GRACE, AND WHO ALSO BELIEVE THAT NATURE HAS NO REVELATION OF SALVATION, MORESO BELIEVE THAT THE INVESTIGATIVE JUDGEMENT IS NOT THE GOSPEL AND EVEN MORE, IT IS NOT TO BE FOUND IN NATURE, BUT THIS IS FAR FROM THE TRUTH! NATURE TEACHES THE WHOLE, GREAT, GRAND ATONEMENT OF WHICH THE INVESTIGATIVE JUDGEMENT IS A PART. HISTORY ALSO BEARS THAT SAME REVELATION, FOR EARTH IS THE LESSON BOOK! (ROMANS 1:16,20) HERE ARE A FEW EXAMPLES OF THE INVESTIGATIVE JUDGEMENT AS SEEN IN NATURE! THE BIBLE TEACHING OF JUDICIAL GRACE GOES THUS: BECAUSE OF SUBJECTIVE SINS MAN MUST SUFFER CONDEMNATION OF DEATH, BUT GOD SUBJECTIVELY GIVES LIFE TO THE SOUL JUSTIFYING HIM. THIS IS FORGIVENESS FOR INWARD SINS. THE MAN IS THEN GIVEN A CHANCE TO COMPLETE REFORM (OR AT LEAST CONTINUE IT TILL DEATH) AND AT THE TIME WHEN HIS NAME IS CALLED IN THE JUDGEMENT, IF THE REFORM IS GENUINE (IN THE CASE OF THOSE WHO DIE OR AT LEAST COMPLETED AMONG THE LIVING SAINTS), THE PAST SINS ARE BLOTTED OUT OR REMOVED FROM HIS RESPONSIBILITY!

THE POINT IN THIS WHICH IS SEEN CLEARLY IN NATURE IS THAT LIFE IS GIVEN FIRST, AND WHEN ASSURED, THE OLD, FORMER PART IS ABOLISHED OR DONE AWAY WITH!

A BRANCH OF A TREE MAY BE INFECTED WITH SOME DISEASE AND BEGIN TO DIE, BUT NEW LIFE COMING INTO THE TREE RECOVERS THE BRANCH, AT WHICH IT NOW HAS LIFE FOR A CERTAIN TIME, THE OLD LEAVES BEGIN TO FALL OFF!

THE LEAVES WITH THE DISEASE DO NOT FALL OFF THE TREE AT THE RECEPTION OF NEW LIFE BY THE BRANCH. RATHER, AFTER THE BRANCH IS CONFIRMED IN ITS NEW LIFE, SO THEN DO THE INFECTED DEAD LEAVES DROP OFF BECAUSE THE HEALING OF THE BRANCH SEVERS THE JOINTS OF THE DEAD LEAVES FROM THE BRANCH! SO LIKEWISE, THE *LIFE OF CHRIST* CONFIRMED IN US BY GOD, CAUSES HIM TO GRACIOUSLY REMIT ALL OUR PAST SINS WHICH HAD REMAINED WHILE WE YET HAD NEW LIFE IN US. THUS, AS GOD WORKS IN NATURE, SO DOES HE WORK WITH US! A SECOND EXAMPLE IS A MAN RECEIVING A CUT ON HIS FINGER WHICH GIVES HIM PAIN! THE PAIN (PAST SINS) REMAINS LONG AFTER HEALING LIFE HAS ALREADY BEGUN IN THE FINGER, AND IT ONLY SUBSIDES WHEN THE HEALING IS BEGUN TO A CERTAIN EXTENT! SO, THE PAST SINS REMAIN AS OUR RESPONSIBILITY UNTIL WE ARE SECURELY HEALED BY SANCTIFICATION! AS THE SCAB FALLS OFF ONLY LONG AFTER THE HEALING HAS BEGUN (FOR IT REMAINED WHILE THE HEALING WAS IN PROCESS), SO ARE THE PAST SINS REMITTED LONG AFTER HEALING HAS BEEN TAKING PLACE! IN HISTORY, THE ACCOUNTS OF ISRAEL SHEW THIS SAME FACT! WHEN THEY SINNED, AN ENEMY CAME AND OPPRESSED THEM. THIS ENEMY IS CONDEMNATION (OR DEATH) FOR SINS! WHEN THEY REPENTED AND WERE SUBJECTIVELY CONVERTED, THE ENEMY (CONDEMNATION) DID NOT AT ONCE LEAVE THEM, BUT THEY REMAINED ONLY UNTIL ISRAEL HAD LEARNT THEIR LESSON OF OBEDIENCE BY SANCTIFICATION. THEN AND ONLY THEN, DID GOD REMOVE THE ENEMY WHICH IS THE FREEING FROM CONDEMNATION BY THE BLOTTING OUT OF PAST SINS! BUT NOT ONLY THAT, THE ENEMIES SYMBOLIZED THE SCAPEGOAT!

IT WAS THE ENEMIES THAT HAD CAUSED ISRAEL TO SIN, AND AS ISRAEL HAD DECLARED HER INNOCENCE BY REPENTANCE AND CONVERSION, SO RETRIBUTION CAME UPON THOSE THAT CAUSED ISRAEL TO SIN, JUST AS IT WILL CERTAINLY FALL UPON SATAN WHO IS THE NEXT IN LINE RESPONSIBLE, AFTER GOD'S PEOPLE HAVE BEEN CLEARED! (JUDGES 2:1-3,11 -16,19-23; JUDGES 3:1- 10,12-30).

THE WORK OF CHRIST IN BLOTTING OUT ALL PAST SINS OR CLEANSING THE SANCTUARY WAS NOT ALWAYS IN PROGRESSION IN THE **LITERAL HEAVENLY SANCTUARY.** IT ACTUALLY STARTED SOME YEARS LATER TO **1798,** A PERIOD DESIGNATED IN THE BOOK OF **DANIEL AS THE** "TIME OF THE END." **IN DANIEL CHAPTER 2** A DREAM IS GIVEN TO THE KING OF BABYLON BY GOD, SHOWING HIM GOD'S INTENTION IN THE HISTORY OF THE EARTH BEGINNING FROM THE EMPIRE OF BABYLON! IN THE STREAM OF HISTORY GOD WORKS OUT MEN'S SALVATION THAT THEY MAY FINALLY BE RATIFIED AS CITIZENS OF GOD'S EVERLASTING **THEODEWELSOISTIC KINGDOM.** THIS WORK IS SUBSTANTIATED BY THE WORK OF THE ATONEMENT WHICH ENDS WITH **JUDICIAL GRACE!** IN **DANIEL CHAPTER 7** THE DEEDS OF THE EMPIRES THAT ARISE AND A STRANGE RELIGIOPOLITICAL POWER IN WHICH CONCENTRATED ALL THE OBTRUSIVENESS OF ALL THE PAST EMPIRES, IS EXPLAINED, AS IT BEARS UPON THE INVESTIGATIVE JUDGEMENT! THIS LAST POWER ESPECIALLY WARS AGAINST GOD'S PEOPLE TO CAUSE THEM TO SIN, BUT THE ATONEMENT IS EFFICACIOUS ENOUGH TO DELIVER THE SAINTS AND TAKE AWAY THE DOMINION OF THIS POWER!

THE INVESTIGATIVE JUDGEMENT, MAKING UP THE SUBJECTS OF GOD'S KINGDOM, TAKES AWAY THE DOMINION OF THIS POWER AND HE IS DESTROYED WHEN SATAN PAYS FOR THE SINS HE CAUSED THE SAINTS TO COMMIT!

DANIEL 8, STARTING WITH MEDO-PERSIA REHASHES THE SAME THING BUT WITH ADDITIONAL NECESSARY DETAILED INFORMATION! A POWER (THE PAPACY OF THE ROMAN CATHOLIC CHURCH) WOULD ARISE FROM THE RUINS OF THE MIGHTY ROMAN EMPIRE, AND THROUGH A MIXTURE OF PAGANISM AND THE FORMS OF CHRISTIANITY WOULD ALMOST ENTIRELY REMOVE THE TRUTHS OF THE ATONEMENT FROM UPON THE FACE OF THE EARTH!

THE TRUTHS OF THE INCARNATION, THE REAL MEANING OF THE SACRIFICIAL CRUCIFIXION, CHRIST AS HEAVENLY HIGH PRIEST IN THE HEAVENLY SANCTUARY, THE CALLING, SUBJECTIVE PASSIVE JUSTIFICATION, SANCTIFICATION IN THE REALM OF SINFREENESS, AND MORESO THE INVESTIGATIVE JUDGEMENT, WERE ALL TRAMPLED UNDER FOOT BY THIS SATANIC POWER, AND WHEN THE QUESTION WAS ASKED AS TO HOW LONG THIS WOULD CONTINUE (VERSE 13), THE ANSWER CONCERNING WHEN THE FINAL WORK OF ATONEMENT, JUDICIAL GRACE, WOULD COMMENCE WAS GIVEN IN VERSE 14! THE PURPOSE OF THIS ANSWER WAS TO REVEAL MANY THINGS, ONE OF WHICH WAS THE FACT THAT THE FULNESS OF TRUTH TRAMPLED BY THE PAPACY WOULD COME BACK UPON THE EARTH IN A CLEAR, UNBROKEN, CHRONOLOGICAL SEQUENCE AFTER THE END OF THE 2300 DAYS! THESE CLEAR TRUTHS WOULD BE IMPLICATIVELY ARRIVED AT BECAUSE OF THE REVELATION OF THE BEGINNING OF THE PROCEEDINGS OF JUDICIAL GRACE IN HEAVEN! THE UNDERSTANDING OF THE **BLOTTING OUT** WOULD LEAD TO THE FACT OF THE **LAW** BEING THE STANDARD OF JUDGMENT, THUS IT MUST BE KEPT AND THIS INCLUDES THE HOLY **SABBATH!**

THUS IT IS THAT **SANCTIFICATION** MUST TOUCH ALL THE ASPECTS OF HUMAN EXISTENCE WHETHER IT IS SOCIAL RELATIONS, ECONOMY, HEALTH OR DRESS STANDARDS, AND IT MUST BE IN THE REALM OF SINFREENESS. THUS **JUSTIFICATION** MUST BE THE BEGINNING OF SINFREE PERFECTION, THE LOVE OF GOD BEING IMPUTED TO THE BELIEVER IN A SUBJECTIVE SENSE! THIS WOULD MEAN THAT THE CALLING MUST GIVE SUBJECTIVE CONVICTION WITHOUT THE MAN YET BEING CONVERTED, HENCE **PREVENIENT GRACE!**

COULD THE WORK OF APPLYING CONVICTION, JUSTIFICATION, SANCTIFICATION AND THE BLOTTING OUT BE DONE WITHOUT AN AGENT? THUS IT WAS SEEN THAT THERE WAS NEEDS BE A **HIGH PRIEST** WHOM THE SCRIPTURES POINTED OUT TO **BE CHRIST!** HE HAD TO HAVE BEEN **RESURRECTED** TO DO THIS, AND TO MEDIATE MERITS HE HAD TO HAVE LAID THEM DOWN IN THE **SACRIFICIAL CRUCIFIXION**, BUT, TO HAVE THE MERITS HE HAD TO HAVE FIRST LIVED A **SINLESS LIFE** IN OBEDIENCE TO THE LAW IN **SINFUL HUMAN FLESH**, THUS HE WAS **INCARNATED!** IT WAS LOVE THAT PROVIDED THE WHOLE PLAN OF ATONEMENT! SO, IT IS THAT AT THE OPENING OF THE SECOND APARTMENT OF THE HEAVENLY SANCTUARY AT THE END OF THE 2300 DAYS TO BEGIN THE WORK OF JUDICIAL GRACE, THAT LIGHT, SHINING DOWN TO THE EARTH ABOUT THE GRAND EVENT, BROUGHT IN ITS TRAIN THE WHOLE, GREAT, GRAND ATONEMENT WHICH WE TEACH NOW! THIS WAS ONE OF THE INTENTIONS OF GOD IN THE 2300 DAYS PROPHECY! AT THE END OF THE 2300 DAYS, THE WORK OF JUDICIAL GRACE WOULD COMMENCE, VINDICATING THE WHOLE SANCTUARY BY ITS TRUTHS OF SALVATION, TO BE JUST AND TRUE, AGAINST THE CLAIMS AND LONG EVIL WORK OF THE PAPACY!

BUT WHAT IS THE 2300 DAYS? IN SCRIPTURE TIME PROPHECIES ARE TO BE EQUATED AS A DAY FOR A YEAR, SO THAT THE 2300 DAYS ARE REALLY 2300 YEARS! BUT WHEN WOULD THIS TIME BEGIN? ACCORDING TO **DANIEL 9:25**, IT WOULD COMMENCE FROM THE GOING FORTH OF THE COMMANDMENT TO RESTORE AND TO BUILD JERUSALEM!

THIS COMMANDMENT IS RECORDED IN **EZRA 7:12-26**, IT WAS DONE BY PERSIAN KING **ARTAXERXES** IN THE AUTUMN OF 457 B.C.B.! 2300 YEARS BEGINNING FROM THAT DATE WILL BRING US TO THE AUTUMN OF THE YEAR 1844, SO THAT IN THAT CONSPICUOUS YEAR, WHILE THE MILLERITES THOUGHT THAT CHRIST WAS RETURNING TO THE EARTH TO CLEANSE IT BY FIRE, IN TRUTH, HE ACTUALLY CAME TO THE SECOND APARTMENT OF THE HEAVENLY SANCTUARY TO BEGIN THE FINAL WORK OF ATONEMENT OR JUDICIAL GRACE! WHEN CHRIST DID NOT APPEAR TO THE EARTH IN 1844, THE MILLERITE MOVEMENT BROKE UP, AND MANY LEFT FAITH IN GOD ALTOGETHER. SOME FORMED NEW RELIGIOUS ORGANIZATIONS, AND SOME, A SMALL COMPANY, WENT AND RESTUDIED THE PROPHECIES, AND WITH THE APPEARANCE OF THE **SPIRIT OF PROPHECY** IN A DYNAMIC SENSE IN THEIR MIDST IN THE PERSON OF ELLEN G. WHITE, THEY DISCOVERED THE BEGINNING OF THE WORK IN THE SECOND APARTMENT OF THE HEAVENLY SANCTUARY! THEIR LABOURS PRODUCED THE SEVENTH DAY ADVENTIST CHURCH WHICH IS PRESENTLY IN APOSTASY BOTH MORALLY AND THEOLOGICALLY, SO THAT GOD IS PRESENTLY RAISING UP **REVIVAL MOVEMENTS** IN THE ORGANIZATION ALL OVER THE WORLD!

IN **TRINIDAD** GOD HAS RAISED UP THE REVIVAL MOVEMENT OF **THUSIA (SDA)**. WE AMONG ALL THE OTHERS HAVE GONE THE FURTHEST IN THE DEVELOPMENT OF THE WHOLE COUNSEL OF GOD AND THERE IS ABOUT TO BE SEEN A GREAT GRAND MISSIONARY CHURCH (THUSIA) DECLARING THE LOVE OF GOD IN THE ATONEMENT ALL OVER THE WORLD TO THE USHERING IN OF THE GREAT SECOND ADVENT OF CHRIST!

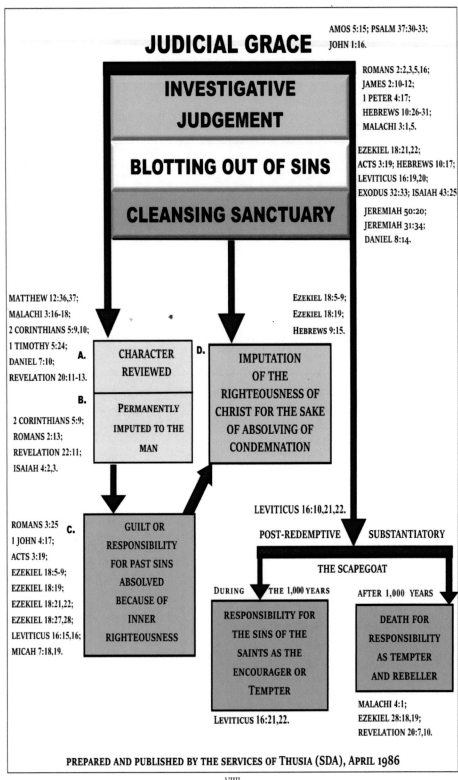

JUDICIAL GRACE

AMOS 5:15; PSALM 37:30-33; JOHN 1:16.

INVESTIGATIVE JUDGEMENT

ROMANS 2:2,3,5,16; JAMES 2:10-12; 1 PETER 4:17; HEBREWS 10:26-31; MALACHI 3:1,5.

BLOTTING OUT OF SINS

EZEKIEL 18:21,22; ACTS 3:19; HEBREWS 10:17; LEVITICUS 16:19,20; EXODUS 32:33; ISAIAH 43:25.

CLEANSING SANCTUARY

JEREMIAH 50:20; JEREMIAH 31:34; DANIEL 8:14.

MATTHEW 12:36,37; MALACHI 3:16-18; 2 CORINTHIANS 5:9,10; 1 TIMOTHY 5:24; DANIEL 7:10; REVELATION 20:11-13.

EZEKIEL 18:5-9; EZEKIEL 18:19; HEBREWS 9:15.

A. CHARACTER REVIEWED

D. IMPUTATION OF THE RIGHTEOUSNESS OF CHRIST FOR THE SAKE OF ABSOLVING OF CONDEMNATION

B. PERMANENTLY IMPUTED TO THE MAN

2 CORINTHIANS 5:9; ROMANS 2:13; REVELATION 22:11; ISAIAH 4:2,3.

ROMANS 3:25; 1 JOHN 4:17; ACTS 3:19; EZEKIEL 18:5-9; EZEKIEL 18:19; EZEKIEL 18:21,22; EZEKIEL 18:27,28; LEVITICUS 16:15,16; MICAH 7:18,19.

C. GUILT OR RESPONSIBILITY FOR PAST SINS ABSOLVED BECAUSE OF INNER RIGHTEOUSNESS

LEVITICUS 16:10,21,22.

POST-REDEMPTIVE   SUBSTANTIATORY

THE SCAPEGOAT

DURING THE 1,000 YEARS

RESPONSIBILITY FOR THE SINS OF THE SAINTS AS THE ENCOURAGER OR TEMPTER

LEVITICUS 16:21,22.

AFTER 1,000 YEARS

DEATH FOR RESPONSIBILITY AS TEMPTER AND REBELLER

MALACHI 4:1; EZEKIEL 28:18,19; REVELATION 20:7,10.

PREPARED AND PUBLISHED BY THE SERVICES OF THUSIA (SDA), APRIL 1986

About The Author

Brother NYRON MEDINA is a modern day Christian Reformer and founding Minister of the Thusia Seventh day Adventist Church in Trinidad and Tobago and its sister churches globally. He was used by YHWH God since the early 1980s to rediscover the authentic understanding of the Gospel as taught by earlier reformers such as the German Christian Reformer Martin Luther.

His discipline over the years in learning spiritual truths in the school of Christ has provided great leadership as the repairer of the breach that had been caused by years of apostasy from original Seventh day Adventism and ancient Apostolic Christianity. His leadership has also served as the restorer of the paths to dwell in, linking us today like a golden chain back to the retrieval of the pure biblical truths of the Gospel of Jesus Christ. No other contemporary Theologian has so accurately recaptured the Gospel, making our church the inheritors of the Reformation and establishing Brother Medina's rightful place in the line of Reformers since the 16th century.

Brother Medina is a prolific writer of Christian religious books, booklets and tracts, long time host and producer with his wife Sis. Dell Medina, of the Television and Radio programs "Escape for thy Life", which are aired in Trinidad and Tobago and St. Vincent and the Grenadines in the Southern and Eastern Caribbean respectively.

If you would like to connect with this author, please call 1-868-373-6108.

To learn more about the Thusia SDA Church and receive our many religious tracts, booklets, video and audio bible studies FREE for download, visit www.thusiasdaevangel.com or call 1-868-624-0446. You are invited to visit our youtube channel: Thusia SDA Gospel for church bible studies, radio programs and television programs.

May God bless you with the sinfree experience today.

Other Publications by Author:

1. Footsteps to Christ

2. The Global Sunday Law

3. Studies in Political Sodomy

4. Studies on Justification Righteousness and Salvation

5. Prophetic Studies

6. Studies on Adventism's Evangelical Gospel

7. The Issue of the Covenants

8. Are Evangelicals True Born Again Christians?

Please contact the Thusia SDA Church at **1 -868-625-0446** for further information on these publications and more.

Made in the USA
Middletown, DE
26 January 2024